HAVENS ACROSS THE SEA

compiled and edited by
Ann Spokes Symonds

ROBERT BOYD PUBLICATIONS

Published by Robert Boyd Publications
260 Colwell Drive, Witney, Oxfordshire OX28 5LW

First edition 1990
Revised edition 2015

ISBN: 978 1 908738 20 2

Copyright © Ann Spokes Symonds

All rights reserved. No part of this publication may be reproduced, stored in a retrieval system or transmitted or recorded in any form by any means, electronic, mechanical, photocopying or otherwise, except for brief extracts for the purpose of review, without the written permission of the copyright owner.

Printed and bound at
Holywell Press Ltd
15-17 Kings Meadow
Ferry Hinksey Road
Oxford OX2 0DP

Dedicated to the Canadian and American families who opened their doors and their hearts and took us in.

'To many British people the fear that their children could be brought up Nazis was worse even than the fear of death. Will you Americans, vowed as you are to freedom .... look for a moment at your children and ask .... what so dreadful a threat would mean to them?'

Dr. Maude Royden: What should a Briton do?, *Christian Century,* 16th April, 1941.

`And not by eastern windows only, When daylight comes, comes in the light; In front the sun climbs slow, how slowly! But westward, look, the land is bright!'

Arthur Hugh Clough,
`Say not the struggle nought availeth'.

CONTENTS

Preface	vii
Foreword	ix
The Planned Exodus	1
British Children at Yale	6
Preparations	14
The First Stage of the Journey	16
The Voyage	21
Quebec	33
Montreal	36
Journey to USA	42
The Divinity School	45
The Open Doors: New Homes and Families	49
The English Children	53
Impressions of America — An Anthology	59
Journeys Home	72
The Extra Bunk	80
The Return to England	83
Homecomings	87

PREFACE

Havens Across the Sea is an account of the evacuation of a party of Oxford children and mothers to Canada and the United States in July, 1940, and their stay with families there in the years which followed. It is composed of recollections and contemporary material contributed by those who made the journey. The introductory chapter called 'The Planned Exodus' is by Ronald Macbeth whose wife and family sailed with the party. There is also an account of 'British children at Yale' by Sidney Lovett, Chaplain of Yale University at the time, which is reprinted by permission from the *Yale Alumni Magazine* of 27th September 1940.

In July, 1990 a reunion - fifty years on - was held in Oxford and some seventy of those who in 1940 sailed to Canada from Liverpool in the Cunard liner *Antonia* attended. All those who expressed an interest in the reunion were invited to send in accounts of their impressions and remembered experiences. Without their contributions, which form part of the text and are individually acknowledged, this book could not have been written. I am therefore most grateful to all the contributors or in the cases where they are no longer alive, to their families.

I am indebted to Diana Halliday for the illustration on page 47. All the other drawings are by the author. My thanks also go to Professor Mark Williamson for permission to reproduce the copy of a page from his passport.

Most of all I should like to thank Helen Macbeth for editing, copying and updating the original text which she typed for the first edition published in 1990. Her skills and patience have been much appreciated.

Ann Spokes Symonds
Oxford, July 2015

FOREWORD

In the 21st century, the world of higher education can often be an intensely competitive one. Nowhere is that more so than in the trans-Atlantic rivalry in which (among many others) Stanford, Harvard and Yale jostle with each other and with Oxford, Cambridge and the LSE for the most talented professors and students. This wonderful little book of recollections reminds us that great bonds of friendship exist between these competing universities and that, in addition to their common purpose of academic scholarship, they can scale great heights of collaboration and support in the face of difficult times.

The book tells the story of a group of families, mothers and children, of Oxford academics who left a battered and beleaguered Britain in 1940 to travel across the Atlantic to safety in the United States. Their destination was New Haven, Connecticut, where the homes of Yale academics, in an act of remarkable support and solidarity, had been opened to receive them. At Yale they would have found much to remind them of home. The gothic architecture of Yale's residential colleges was conspicuously based on their Oxford counterparts. The lawns and quadrangles of Saybrook and Branford resemble those of Hertford and Christ Church. But much would have been unfamiliar, especially the sweltering summers and brutal New England winters. Most importantly they found a haven of peace and abundant provisions, very different from war-torn and rationing-restricted Britain.

The links between Yale and Oxford remain strong. Every year a significant number of students make the trek from one institution to the other learning from and contributing to the strength of their academic endeavours. The much beloved President of Yale,

Kingman Brewster, became later in his career the Master of University College, Oxford. The longest serving Yale President of the last many decades, Rick Levin, often points to his formative time at Merton College, Oxford and his philosophy tutorials with Isiah Berlin. My own career took the opposite direction from the position of Provost and Professor of Chemistry at Yale to become Vice-Chancellor of Oxford.

All of these links, and especially the times described in this book, remind us of how important universities are to the health and future of each other and the role that they play in representing the very best of their host countries in times of great national and international need.

Andrew D. Hamilton
Vice-Chancellor, University of Oxford
August, 2015

THE PLANNED EXODUS

By Ronald Macbeth

Background
In the Spring of 1940 and after a severe winter the war in the West had drifted into a condition sometimes called the phoney war. On May 10th in splendid weather the Germans began their lightning attack through Holland, Belgium and France. By June 1st the British Army in Europe had been either evacuated via Dunkirk or captured. Invasion of this country seemed to be extremely likely.

The Dominions had come in on our side early in the war, but in the U.S.A. traditional isolationism combined with a population of mixed European origin had not at that stage led to a general sympathy with Britain. The scene now changed, and the Transatlantic peoples began to suggest that British children be sent over to them for the duration. In the United States a 'Committee for the Care of European Children' was set up as a nationwide organisation, and this appears to have had branches or affiliated bodies over much of that country.

In New Haven (Connecticut) such a Committee was set up largely by members of the Yale Faculty and indeed was called 'The Yale Faculty Committee for receiving Oxford and Cambridge University Children'.

[See article by Sidney Lovett, page 6].

Trinity Term in Oxford
John Fulton, Professor of Physiology at Yale, had been nominated to make personal contacts at Oxford and Cambridge, with the general invitation to the two British Universities to send their children to Yale. He had been a Rhodes Scholar and later a Fellow of Magdalen, and his approaches were made by cable on June 6th to medical friends and colleagues. At Oxford

his contact initially was with Hugh Cairns, Professor of Surgery, and himself a past Rhodes Scholar. Cairns was maintaining the dual role of Professor and Brigadier in the Army Medical Service, and he passed on the message to Howard Florey, Professor of Pathology, who was another Rhodes Scholar.

In his turn Florey got into touch with Carleton Allen, the Warden of Rhodes House, and correspondence thereafter was conducted between Allen and Fulton. From then onwards Carleton Allen became the king-pin in the arrangements and, because he was a barrister, his skills were particularly welcomed. Meetings of Senior Members of the University were hastily organised at Rhodes House, and in principle Yale's generous offer was immediately accepted. Cambridge asked for time to consider. Meanwhile a similar invitation from Toronto University had been relayed via the Dean of Christ Church (yet another Rhodes Scholar) and at some stage an invitation from Swarthmore became associated with the one from Yale. All these invitations emanated spontaneously from across the Atlantic.

Additionally various people had had personal invitations from friends in Canada and the U.S. It was thought sensible that if a mass exodus of children were arranged all of these groups of invitees should travel together.

The Meetings at Rhodes House
How we parents heard about these is, after this lapse of time, uncertain. Probably it was by word of mouth in our various colleges. The meetings were conducted by Allen with help from Dean Lowe of Christ Church. They were serious to the point of being soul-searching but they were never either argumentative or hysterical. Some of us felt strongly that we would not wish to have our children subjected to Nazi occupation; others in

Rhodes House, Oxford

the end felt that the trauma of separation would be too great. The question of air-raids really hardly came into it. If a bomb had one's address on it, that would be that. Unfortunately, no records were kept of the meetings which took place at 5 p.m. on hot summer days or sometimes on a Sunday morning.

At an early stage a solicitor attended the meetings and he was a great help on matters of currency, passports and immigration. When it became clear that a sizeable party would hope to travel a representative from a local Travel agency also was there. Two important questions soon cropped up. The first was in relation to our definition of a child, and my recollection is that we excluded people over the age of 15 but decided that there should be no lower limit. The second query was whether some mothers could be included in the party. It was agreed that, provided the sponsors were of the same mind, mothers of small children or large families should be given the chance of going. The sponsoring bodies welcomed this. Each individual could take £10 in cash and needed a valid passport. On the American side there was some difficulty with the immigration authorities who were sticky about admitting aliens as long-term visitors.

[See the Yale account]. However, people could be so admitted by visiting from Canada. So a ship bound for Canada and landing the human cargo there might circumvent this bit of red tape. In part it did.

At that time comparatively few passenger ships were crossing the Atlantic, and attacks by U-boats were intensifying. Furthermore, the enemy was claiming - possibly correctly in some instances - that these same ships carried gold bullion and other important cargo, and therefore were justifiable targets.

By dint of concentrated work it was found possible to book 'Tourist' places for 125 children and 25 mothers on SS Antonia, due to sail for Montreal early in July. In the event some of the places became vacant and were hastily filled by people from Cambridge and elsewhere. In retrospect it seems astonishing that the whole project got under way in a matter of three weeks. On Monday, 8th July, 1940, therefore, the group set forth from Oxford and sailed on the 9th/10th. Mrs. Kitty Burn, besides coping with her own four children, travelled as party nurse in Guy's Hosipital uniform and Kenneth Franklin, the Medical School Dean, went as courier and general liaison officer.

The Trust Fund
At an early stage in our meetings at Rhodes House the question had been raised of how we might be able to repay the hosts of our families, and Carleton Allen went to a great deal of trouble about this after the party had left. There is a considerable correspondence between him and the Treasury. Apart from the whole question of maintenance, we - with long-term optimism - wanted to establish that the cost of repatriation should not fall on the foster-parents. To set up a Trust Fund seemed to be the answer.

Basically the Treasury's position was that neither then nor in the future could money be earmarked for the direct benefit of the hosts or their families. A Trust Fund would be permitted for utilisation after the war was over, but with the important proviso that individuals should not benefit.

A question was asked in the House of Commons about the matter and thereafter the Treasury's attitude was somewhat modified. We were then told that the money could be spent in this country for the benefit of organised bodies, such as Universities, after the war's end.

By 1946 the Fund had accumulated £17,000 and Yale generously added the residue of its own Trust Fund - about £7,000. The trustees of our Fund set aside a sum for the utilisation of Toronto University in Oxford, and as a major project in 1947 they entertained Americans at the July Summer School in Oxford - sixty teachers drawn from the schools all over the U.S.A. which our children had attended.

It turned out that we need not have worried about the payment for repatriation. The families returned sporadically over the years and we were all able to pay in sterling on this side.

RONALD MACBETH

BRITISH CHILDREN AT YALE

by Sidney Lovett
[Reprinted, by permission, from the
Yale Alumni Magazine, 27 September, 1940]

ABOUT Commencement time, June, 1940, the idea was born. The clearest claim to parenthood may be established by half a dozen faculty members who put their names to an initial statement of purpose circulated among their colleagues. I, myself, was present on Friday, June 21, at the home of Dr. and Mrs. Charles-E. A. Winslow when the enterprise was christened. It was given the mouth-filling name, Yale Faculty Committee for Receiving Oxford and Cambridge University Children. An anonymous gift of one thousand dollars marked the initial monetary contribution to the growth and development of the project, now grown to lusty youth and commanding financial resources totaling over forty thousand dollars.

Dwight Memorial Chapel
and Harkness Tower
Yale University

Two important moves were made the week of June 16. One was to measure faculty response to the suggestion of receiving into their homes children of Oxford and Cambridge University families. The reaction to this proposal was immediate and generous. Cards and letters received in reply to an initial inquiry totalled 390, with "beds" provided for 247 children. Financial help was promised by many who could not include youngsters in their homes. Simultaneous with this action on the home front, invitations to receive and care for one hundred children were cabled by Dr. John F. Fulton *(Minnesota and Magdalen, '21)* to Mr. C. K. Allen, Warden of Rhodes House, Oxford University, and to Mr. Will Spens of Cambridge University by Professor Samuel B. Hemingway. Thankful replies were duly received from both Universities. It soon became clear that Oxford was preparing to take up our offer. Cambridge asked for time in which to give the matter further consideration.

Several important operations marked the summer months. First in order was the quest for a golden fleece, the prize in this instance being a corporate affidavit approved by the Department of State to enable the Oxford party, already instructed to clear away to Canada as soon as possible, to proceed as a group to this country. On Monday, June 24, contact was established with both the International Migration Service and the United States Committee for the Care of European Children, with offices in New York City. Words are not sufficient to praise the patience and skill with which Mrs. William Burns listened and gave answers to the many queries put to her by a very bewildered but persistent inquirer representing the Yale Faculty Committee. Under her guidance, certain facts began to take shape. It would be wise to incorporate the Yale Faculty Committee under the laws of the State of Connecticut. This was done June 28,

1940, through the good offices of Mr. Arthur L. Corbin, Jr., of Watrous, Hewitt, Gumbart and Corbin. Among other things, this timely incorporation aided the chairman in securing a ten-thousand-dollar gift from an anonymous source outside New Haven, which doubled our resources as of July 1.

Our committee early became an integral part of the United States Committee and subject to all its privileges and responsibilities. Connection was made with the Children's Center of Hamden, which was designated by the United States Committee to supervise the selection of homes for our Oxford party and determine their proper placement. An information sheet was sent to all prospective foster parents, returnable to the Children's Center as the basis for personal interviews between the signers and the placement workers.

On July 11 the following cable came to hand from Mr. C. K. Allen of Oxford University:

"GOODS DISPATCHED. JAMES IN TOUCH WITH CUNARD ABOUT ARRIVAL. CONSIDERABLE CHANGES IN LISTS FOR VARIOUS REASONS BUT ALL PLACES FILLED. . ."

This meant that our party was actually on the way. With over $20,000 in hand, a good sized list of foster homes under investigation or already approved, McGill University ready to receive the party on arrival in Canada, the Sterling Divinity Quadrangle and the Children's Center prepared for their comfort and convenience in New Haven pending final settlement in private homes, it only remained, in conjunction with the United States Committee, to secure from the Departments of Justice and State the corporate affidavit which would enable the party, supplied with visitors' visas, to cross the border. Another trip to Washington by the chairman on Friday, July 12, was highly significant. Through the good offices of Mr.

Dean G. Acheson, '15, access was provided to Mr. Henry Hart, Jr., Assistant to Solicitor General Francis Biddle. Mr. Hart proved to be an accomplished fleece-hunter in his own right. He was possessed of practical wisdom and imagination, in the proper proportions. Our party, actually on the water and soon to arrive in Canada, gave him something definite to work on. From the day of our meeting until Tuesday, July 23, things began to move both in Washington and in New York City. The chairman slipped into a comfortable chair, now in New Haven, now in New York, while the lawyers and government officials engaged in some first-rate tape-cutting. With the result that on Tuesday morning, July 23, two days after the safe arrival of our party in Montreal, word came from Washington and was relayed to the United States Consul in Montreal that the corporate affidavit was granted our party by the State Department. Thus a precedent was established to cover the possible entrance of subsequent groups of refugees to this country under the auspices of the United States Committee, and the way open to our particular party of Oxford mothers and children to entrain for New Haven at their earliest convenience, equipped with the proper credentials.

Under some such title as *The Rover Boys in Canada,* it is to be hoped that Messrs. Fulton and Hemingway may be persuaded to describe in detail the reception of the Oxford University faculty mothers and children. No two gentlemen could have extended to the British evacuees the welcome of Yale University, faculty, alumni, and friends in a more convincing manner. Mr. Joseph Berger, of Madison, Connecticut, acted as official courier, dealing in a most effective and expeditious way with customs and immigration authorities. McGill University, from its principal to its porters, was instant in friendly ministrations. Mr. Homer Byington, U. S. Consul in Montreal, proved the soul of consideration and courtesy. Dr. Kenneth Franklin, acting dean of the Medical School, Oxford, who shepherded the party overseas, turned into an admirable liaison officer between his wards and their New World friends. Not of his choosing was a stowaway measles germ brought out of England in the person of one of his young charges. There was an especially dark hour in the night of July 23, when it looked as though the whole party might be indefinitely detained in Canada for medical reasons. Fine cooperation over the telephone by public health authorities in New Haven and Montreal enabled the group, minus the active measles, to entrain as scheduled on the morning of July 24, subject to quarantine and other health precautions to be undertaken on arrival.

Through the good offices of President Seymour and Dean Weigle and the Board of Directors of the Children's Center in Hamden, Connecticut, the Sterling Divinity Quadrangle and the baby house of the Children's Center were ready and staffed for temporary occupancy by the evacuees. Mr. and Mrs. Burton A. MacLean and Mrs. O. H. Mowrer, with a corps of young men and women largely recruited from faculty families, took over the care of a few mothers with their own children and all the unattached youngsters at the Divinity School. Mrs. Marrian Gilbert acted as matron of the majority of mothers with very young children at the Children's Center. A heat wave of unprecedented torridness in these parts, routine physical checkups with added inoculations, the limitations of quarantine regulations, sporadic cases of measles, failed to break the morale of our overseas friends or to check the rapid growth of Anglo-American cordiality, marked even by the free exchange of British and Yankee slang. The fine courtesy and patience of our English guests under conditions not only new but often embarrassing, excites one's unqualified admiration in retrospect.

Within a month all were established in foster homes.

The United States Committee for the Care of European Children with which our faculty organization was associated from the start was required by the U. S. Government to entrust all child placement to an accredited social agency. In line with this policy the Children's Center of Hamden, of which Mr. Byron Hacker is the director, was charged with the allocation of our Oxford party. Three members of the Yale Committee sat with the placement council in a purely advisory capacity. Our invitation last June was extended to one hundred children each from both Oxford and Cambridge Universities between the ages of five and sixteen years. On the basis of this expectation a large number of foster homes were solicited, and the response was generous. Of the Oxford party twenty-one mothers and children stayed with friends and relatives in Canada. Eight mothers with their eighteen children plus eleven unattached children have been consigned by previous arrangement to persons and homes in this country outside of our committee's auspices. Our immediate placement problem was thus reduced to the settlement of seventeen mothers with thirty-seven children belonging to them and thirty-nine unattached youngsters into something like three or four times as many homes that were open to them.

Anything approaching a complete distribution of the party was mathematically impossible, short of physical dismemberment. The problem of placement presented psychological as well as numerical considerations. Mothers accompanied by their own children had to be settled, for the most part, in family units. Children unattached to parents had very often to be kept together and not too far removed from other family units. A group of four might be divided between two foster homes but not spread over four. This made necessary a concentration of the party in a relatively small number of available foster homes. The wisdom of keeping the whole party somewhat geographically centered precluded our use of many homes at some distance from New Haven. All prospective homes and foster parents were subject to interview by child placement workers. Undoubtedly this put a momentary premium on the members of our faculty and community who were near by. Acquaintance with guest mothers and children was both desirable and permissible, but no sponsor was encouraged to pick and choose. Foster parents who could guarantee full support of adults or children assigned to them and those who could not were given equal consideration by the placement committee. It was hoped that the final allocation would reflect as wide a distribution as possible between university departments and professional ranking.

It is not within the scope of this report to express the gratitude of the Yale Faculty Committee to the many individuals who have helped further this particular venture in human relations. One may single out two particular groups of persons for especial thanks. The many individuals, in New Haven and outside, whose good offices as foster parents were solicited but not as yet utilized deserve and have the full appreciation of the committee. Some replacements of the present group will be inevitable this fall and winter. Individual children are still expected from overseas. Our books are not yet closed and we shall count on the continued co-operation of this group. Without anything approaching a general solicitation of funds, between forty and fifty thousand dollars have been contributed to the committee by donors, known and anonymous, and representing members of the faculty, citizens of the community, alumni and friends of the University.There came out from Oxford last month a letter addressed to Dr. John F. Fulton and signed by several dons whose wives and children are at present in our care. In part it reads as follows:

"Having heard from our families and from Dr. Franklin of the unbounded kindness and solicitude which you and your organization have bestowed on our wives and children, we desire to express to you our deep appreciation of your unstinted aid and care. We are happy to accept your pledges of friendship as a generous gift not only to ourselves as parents, not only to the University which has established enduring ties between us, but, above all, to our country in its defence of those beliefs, traditions, and institutions which are the common concern of our two nations. We feel that we can never adequately repay all your good offices, though we are resolved to make such return as may be within our power; meanwhile we wish to assure you that we are deeply comforted to know that our wives and children are the guests of those who have offered so spontaneously and so liberally the hospitality not merely of friends or benefactors, *but,* if you will permit us so to think of you, of kindred."

Sidney Lovett,
University Chaplain,
Chairman of the Yale Faculty
Committee for Receiving
Oxford and Cambridge University Children

PREPARATIONS

Life at Oxford during warm June days continued much as usual. Yellow signs pointing to ARP (Air Raid Precautions) posts and black-out curtains were often the only external evidence of the emergency. In the summer number of *The American Oxonian,* the writer of the Oxford letter explained: 'Old rowing men will realize that it would take nothing less than a German submarine in the Isis to interfere with Eights Week.'

'The preparations that Summer' writes Felicity Hugh-Jones Arnott, 'seemed like endless shopping for warm vests and such (abandoned by our hosts in centrally-heated houses) and the provision of large blue fibre suitcases painted with an identifying yellow band. I still have one of them complete with typed list inside the lid, my father carefully translating plimsolls into sneakers. I remember Mummy telling me that public lavatories were called comfort stations but it was our Welsh nanny who, discovering my innocence the night before we left, gave me a quick run-down on the facts of life. I have always been grateful to her for that. I was 12 years old. My chief concern was that we were to be allowed only one small attaché case each for personal belongings and what to put in it? I packed and re-packed. In the end I settled for some favourite books, my teddy bear, my microscope and my tonsils. I'd had them out the year before and had insisted on taking them away from the Radcliffe with me...'

'As I was unlucky in the mother's ballot', recalls Betty Hume-Rothery, 'Jennifer, then only 5, and her cousin John Fea, aged 8, were going alone till one family's measles made a vacancy for me. Though few days now remained I then had to spend one precious one in London joining a long queue at the Foreign office in a possibly fruitless quest for a permit to leave the country. However, when the tired-faced but courteous young man whose office I eventually penetrated took one look at the fair curly head and smiling face in Jennifer's passport he just said: 'This child needs her mother with her' and signed my form. So I went with the rest.'

'One day our parents came back from a meeting at Rhodes House (writes Ann Spokes) and said to my brother and me: "I'm afraid we have a disappointment for you." We were very worried for fear it meant we were not going after all. In the event it was just to say that instead of going to stay in Canada, as originally planned, we were to go to the U.S.A. We were both delighted to hear this.'

Parents were asked to take away from school every child who was going on the voyage. There was measles at one of the schools and it was important that we were germ-free for the journey. This extra holiday was certainly for us one of the best parts of the waiting period.

In June parents signed papers agreeing to the evacuation to Canada and the U.S.A. of their child (or children) and authorising the foster-parents to take decisions of any kind on their behalf. In July both parents of all children going to America signed another form consenting to their children proceeding to the United States for indefinite residence, *'there to be received into the custody of a foster-parent to be nominated by Professor John Fulton residing at Yale University, New Haven, Connecticut, who has assumed full responsibility for the maintenance and support of our children.'*

THE FIRST STAGE OF THE JOURNEY

Oxford to Liverpool

The majority of family partings took place at Oxford railway station. Some fathers, however, were already serving in the Armed Forces or on Government service and a written farewell had to suffice. Four-year old Martin Hugh-Jones, for instance, received this letter from his father:-

>LONDON, JUNE 25th 1940
>DARLING BOY,
>THIS IS A LITTLE NOTE
>TO BRING YOU YOUR DADDY'S LOVE
>ON YOUR BIG ADVENTURE.
>JUST SAY TO YOURSELF, WILL
>YOU, ' DADDY LOVES ME VERY
>MUCH' AND BE SURE THAT IT
>WON'T BE VERY LONG BEFORE
>THERE IS ANOTHER BIG SHIP FOR
>ALL OF US.
> ALWAYS YOUR LOVING
>   DADDY
>xoxoxoxoxoxoxo
>oxoxoxoxoxoxox

Martin's three sisters were also sent letters and Felicity writes: 'When our children show horror at the idea of our being sent away, I remember those letters and get some inkling of what it must have been like for our parents.'

For many of us, the goodbyes at Oxford, on that warm 8th July Monday, although sad and tearful, were soon forgotten in the excitement of the journey and thoughts of the sea voyage to come. In those days, not many families took holidays abroad and it was, for most of the children, their first visit away from the British Isles. Felicity Hugh-Jones Arnott again:-

'The day we left was like all that summer, wonderfully hot and sunny. At Oxford station it was all hugger-mugger, picnic lunch provided: an outing from which we would all return home that night.'

Some younger children, who were accompanied by their mothers, were surprised that 'Daddy' was not coming too.

Ellie Vickers (née Bourdillon), remembers:-

'As our train pulled away from family and friends…I apparently leaned out of the carriage window and called: "Wouldn't it be fun if we were torpedoed!" She continues:- 'I suppose this summed up the state of mind of the younger travellers - it was an adventure, fun at that stage because we were a party and leaving home hadn't made itself felt, and we had no idea how long the separation would last. One thought in round terms of "a year or so". In my case it was almost six years.'

For mothers, attempting in vain to keep a stiff upper lip in front of the children, it was far worse. One of these, Ethelwyn Goodwin, mother of Richard, aged 4, and five-month old Rodney, wrote to her husband that evening: 'I am sorry I broke down for a minute, but I was not as red-eyed as some mothers. Sweetheart - I love you so much and I feel quite happy and confident about going and I know that soon we shall be together again. Take care of your good self.'

The Oxford families had left their homes for the railway station at about 8.15 am, although for those who lived outside the City it had meant an earlier start. The train left the station amid the waves of parents at 9.30 a.m.

'I still remember my mother,' writes Ann Spokes,' in a kelly-green dress, waving from the end of the platform and recall that I was proud of the fact that she had run the fastest and thus could be seen from the window of our carriage at the end of the train long after everyone else.'

At Banbury, the first stop, little Susan Lawson, aged 5, asked: "Is this Canada yet?"

Many of the younger children believed we would arrive in America the next day if not that night. Others did not even know where we were going.

'I was ten when we left for America,' recalls Dr. Heather Ashton (née Champion). For some reason I had no idea where we were going. I asked my big brother (Jimmy Champion) aged 12.

"I think we might be going to Australia or New Zealand. If you sit on a tree stump there, the ants come and eat you from the bottom up."

In the way of small sisters, I actually believed this piece of brotherly intelligence all the way until our arrival.'

The train made scheduled stops after Banbury at Leamington, Birmingham, Wolverhampton, Shrewsbury and Birkenhead, but there were unexplained halts in the middle of countryside.

'Though I started with an almost empty carriage,' wrote Ethelwyn Goodwin to her husband, 'I had not gone far before being joined by four girls so we were a houseful. I was really proud of the boys. They were just marvellous - considering the journey was hot and we were about an hour late - an hour's wait at Wolverhampton.' Baby Rodney had been placed in a hammock 'and we had a procession in the corridor to see it.'

At Birkenhead we left the train and crossed the river by paddle-steamer, arriving in Liverpool at 3.30 p.m.

Rankin Hall
It was at Rankin Hall, Liverpool University where we spent our last night in England. Formerly a men's hostel, it had already been taken over by University Hall,

a hall of residence for women students, because the latter's premises had been requisitioned, on the outbreak of war, for the Postal Censorship Organisation.

Here the friendly students who received us had even prepared a nursery with two playpens and toys strewn about and the mothers were given cups of tea. At the time, we assumed that this hospitality had been devised especially for our one night's stay but in fact for much of that summer vacation Rankin Hall served as a transit camp for children being evacuated across the Atlantic and many of the students stayed 'up' (an Oxford term) to help with the organisation.

Assembled in the dining hall, we were allocated our rooms. Whilst mothers and young children had smaller rooms of their own, groups of children shared larger ones; for instance, eleven boys slept in one room. Most of us slept on the floor on mattresses with a couple of blankets but no pillows or sheets. We were given milk and biscuits and even the group of older girls aged betwen 13 and 15 were expected to be in bed by 7.30 p.m. As many of them were good friends already they talked until 10.30 p.m.

Daphne Dunkin (née James) remembers 'weeping on the turn of a magnificent stairway the night we spent in Liverpool' and Felicity Hugh-Jones Arnott, who had charge of three younger siblings, sisters of 9 and 3 and 4 year-old Martin, recalls: 'the four of us perched in our beds alone in a still-sunlit dormitory. I think that was the bleak moment when I realised that nothing would be the same again.

Liverpool formalities

Tuesday, 9th July
Having risen at 7 a.m. it was 10.30 a.m. before the coaches (charabancs in those days) collected us from Rankin Hall and took us to the Cunard buildings.

There, everyone was packed into a small room and, after an hour of waiting, all the babies were yelling and the older children were bored. By comparison it was exciting to be summoned into an adjoining room where two men were sitting with our passports, looked at the photographs and then looked at us and let us walk out again.

There was further waiting in the charabancs before our passports were returned to us and we finally walked up the gangway onto the liner *Antonia*. From on board ship Ethelwyn Goodwin wrote to her husband:- 'We are off soon after a dreadful morning of waits. Even Richard cried with weariness and Rodney was howling as well for about ten minutes - then they brightened up and we all feel better after lunch. The worst is over now - all the morning was hell.'

Cunard's liner, Antonia.

THE VOYAGE

Although ostensibly travelling 'tourist' or third-class on this one-funnelled Cunarder, the space allocated to the Oxford party was so deep in the bowels of the ship that 'steerage' would have been a more appropriate description. Soon after boarding, everyone was handed a berthing card by Dr. Franklin which had on it the number of one's cabin. Some of the cabins were about the size of a railway compartment, others - mainly for mothers and children - were a litle larger. None had portholes. Even some of the children, who had never been on a liner before, found the space surprisingly restricted.

'The amount of room for moving about the cabin,' wrote Felicity Hugh-Jones in the diary-letter she wrote to her parents, ' is about as much as there is in the china cupboard.'

Most of any spare space there might have been in the square, onto which the cabins faced, was taken up by one or two mysterious crates, the size of three or four cabins, which were rumoured to contain gold bullion bound for Fort Knox.

Ethelwyn Goodwin to her husband: 'As you had warned me about the cabin, I was not surprised by their pokiness - but many were and Mrs. L. burst into tears. Many of us have wished for a cinematograph of the show to enable our husbands to get a glimpse of the amazing conditions and the way we are living - but perhaps it is as well you never see it. The first day was an awful muddle - and the sight of so many children appalled the Cunard people - stewards. Our cabins were all in one block round a big square...You can imagine the atmosphere - not a porthole open in the whole of the ship because of black-out conditions.

'Oxford would certainly collapse at the sight of D deck - lines of nappies - suitcases in piles outside cabins round the square - mothers bathing and feeding babies in each corner, children playing snap in groups, toddlers pushing animals and engines in and out of the mob.'

Ann Huckstep (née Macbeth) also remembers 'Mothers breastfeeding babies (a phenomenon new to me). I can even mention names.'

Felicity Hugh-Jones wrote at the time: 'We are woken at 6 a.m. by the crying of babies and outside the cabins is...like a flag day with nappies drying. The only air we get is what blows down from the deck - the heat was unbearable.'

Ethelwyn Goodwin described the conditions:- 'The boat is a very old one and rather dirty and though it has nurseries it is not very convenient. There are not half enough bathrooms for the third class and it is quite a walk to them. Then the deck and dining-rooms are a mile from the lavies for the children - and from the cabins. I did not expect much so don't grumble like some of us do - in fact it has really been rather fun and the only thing to do is laugh at it. But the noise!!! After getting up in the morning and before breakfast the tinies career round the square shouting merrily all with voices as loud as Richard's.'

Although the *Antonia* had sailed from Liverpool harbour on the evening of 9th July it was not until about 6.30 p.m. on the 10th that she left the mouth of the Mersey. The children were anxious to be on deck to say farewell to England but there were many who missed the critical moment because it was bath time for the little ones. Older girls' duties included giving a nightly bath to the younger children and both Cynthia Sever and Helen Somerset, for instance, were bathing the Phelps-Browns and the younger Hugh-Jones children at the time. Bathing was a nightly ritual. The eldest Hugh-Jones, Felicity, recalls:- 'The four of us would pile together into a big bath - hot sea water with special soap that left you feeling sticky.'

At the time of departure, however, Felicity was one of the luckier ones who was on deck at the time. In her letter home she wrote:- 'At 6 p.m. the tide began to run out and the boat began to run 'til her stern faced the sea; then at 6.20 p.m. her anchor was pulled up and with the Skirmisher [one of the tugs] with an immense rope...she nosed our boat round 'til they faced the sea. Then we went out under our own steam.'

However, even then there were further delays and the need to wait for orders from Liverpool meant that we were once more at anchor. A man shouted from the nearby destroyer D 25 to explain why. The final sailing went largely unnoticed as children began to amuse themselves on board.

As the days went by everyone became used to the daily routine which included a morning medical examination given by Dr. Franklin. It was not arduous and was often no more than a look from both Dr. and Mrs. (also a doctor) Franklin. The kindness and care of the two doctors were particularly remembered by Ellie Bourdillon Vickers and Felicity Hugh-Jones Arnott. Notices of information were plastered on the outside of the Franklin's cabin door. Then there was Kitty Burn, who had her own four children with her, who was a registered nurse and wore Guy's Hospital uniform, 'bustling about in starched navy blue and white', Ann Macbeth Huckstep recalls, 'like some latter-day Florence Nightingale, apparently tireless, ministering to our needs.'

Children under 14 were made to rest on their beds each afternoon whilst older children were allowed to take their rests on deck chairs above. There was sometimes a shortage of chairs and we can remember being unceremoniously turfed out of them by some of the refugees from Germany and Austria, large numbers of whom were on board. One afternoon, an older mother in our party, who liked to see that all the children behaved themselves, said to a boy of about ten who was still on deck:- 'Shouldn't you be on your bed? Go down below at once.' However, it turned out that the child was not a member of our party. Inevitably, an account of this mistake was passed round among the older children and heard with unconcealed amusement.

The misery of a 'real swell'
There are few who do not remember Friday, 12th July when the *Antonia* hit exceedingly rough seas just to the west of Ireland. Even some of the stewards and stewardesses were affected. A group of girls spent the day between rail and deck chair not caring whether they lived or died. The record for being sick was 16 times. Peter Spokes, Neil Maidment, and five-month old Rodney Goodwin and some other babies were among the few boys who were not sick. Cynthia Sever and Wendy Clarke were the girl survivors.

'The sailors said it was a real swell,' wrote Ann Spokes in her diary, 'and they explained: "our deck was especially rocky because we had big heavy railway-like crates on board it".'

In the bows the waves came over the ship. Only nine people were at lunch in the large dining room which normally served two sittings. It was particularly hard for mothers who had to think of others beside themselves.

'I spent the day lying on my bed,' wrote Mrs. Goodwin to her husband, 'rising only for feeds and to minister to Richard. Oh, darling it was awful - I just wept in the afternoon and cursed the day I ever attempted this crusade - I was so exhausted trying to produce milk from nothing with no food and drink...'

By evening most had become used to the rocking of the ship but it was several days before the most badly affected passengers were able to eat normal meals or feel comfortable below deck. The appropriate children's rhyme summed up the day:-

> "My breakfast is over the ocean
> My luncheon is over the sea
> My tummy's in such a commotion
> Don't bring any supper to me."

Torpedoes

Our convoy, which had been escorting us from the mouth of the Mersey, left us at about 10.30 that night when we were some 800 miles from land. From then on we were out on our own. Dr. Franklin explained to us that we were now supposed to be out of danger of enemy activity. Nevertheless, everyone was still instructed to carry their life-jackets with them wherever they went. Though not always observed by the children, this was no doubt a sensible precaution.

Reports printed later in July in the *Oxford Times* and *Oxford Mail* read:

> *The liner was four days out in the Atlantic when an enemy submarine fired two torpedoes at it. They both missed, but the escape was narrow for one of the 'tin fish' passed within six feet of the boat. Speed was increased but the danger was past, for the submarine did not dare surface because of the warships in charge of the convoy. Depth charges were dropped but whether they were successful is not known.*

A later report which appeared in the (London) *Daily Mail* on 22nd July quotes one of the ship's engineers as saying: 'There was only one thing we could do - cram on speed. We certainly made the boilers wheeze.'

There is no record of the actual date of this occurrence and although there were rumours not all the children knew about it at the time. Bobby Franklin (now Elizabeth Symon) recalls:- 'Our ship was a Cunarder in convoy. An enemy torpedo almost hit us but went vertical instead of horizontal as it neared us. We still felt a terrific jolt.'

Wendy Clarke, one of the few eye witnesses, remembers: 'hauling small boys from the stern deck-railing just as a torpedo passed yards astern of us. Depth charges thrown in white canisters over the side to explode with spine-jarring crumps. Had we hit a rock?'

Unfortunately, we have no accounts written at the time. We feared the censor's scissors would spoil our letters home and had been told to include nothing about such matters.

Ethelwyn Goodwin's husband wrote to his wife from Oxford on 24th July:- 'In Monday's edition of the *Oxford Mail* there was a story that your ship had been attacked by a submarine when you were four days out in the Atlantic...but most people in the common-room were inclined to treat this with suspicion.'

Helen Somerset Lock writes in retrospect:- 'Concern had been shown about our education and accents but little consideration, apparently, had been given to the extreme danger of an unescorted ship crossing the Atlantic - rumours abounded of U-boats and torpedoes. Were we incredibly lucky to have escaped the fate of *The City of Benares,* also evacuating children, which was sunk later that summer?'

Felicity Hugh-Jones, aged 12, writing to her father on Thursday, 11th July:- 'I don't want you to worry 'cos I'm going to look after Martin and Jenny and Zig and myself [the four were on their own] very carefully, and I want you to look after Mummy and Mummy to look after you, and I want you to remember if anything does happen to us, we will always meet together in Heaven, that should always be the belief of Everybody, and God is merciful. But I don't want to depress you 'cos I'm sure the War will end soon.'

There were also worries about what would happen

on arrival and her letter continues:- 'I would like it if you would write out a list of things for me to remember, 'cos I may find it difficult in a strange country in spite of the discussions we had about it.'

Activities

News from England was scanty. The BBC broadcasts were only relayed in the first-class but the important items in each 9 p.m. (British time) bulletin were printed out and stuck on the third-class notice board. Felicity noticed the fact that 'the German invasion of Britain begins on Friday' but she also wrote that she thought that was 'a bit optimistic of the Nazis.' 'Having nothing else to do,' she recorded, near the end of the voyage, 'I carved **H-J, 1940** on the foredeck so that the ship will carry it for ever.'

After half a century one tends to remember the happy times on board. Felicity remembers the liner *Antonia* as a great adventure. She loved the sea 'and travelling so long and far was exciting. I can't recall how long we were at sea: I think I would have gone on happily for ever.'

The efforts of a group of good-natured Rhodes scholars who organised deck games, treasure hunts and team games are remembered with pleasure and Wendy Clarke recalls them 'entertaining children with songs and stories, rousing teenage passions.' The Rhodes scholars divided the children into groups according to age; for instance one group was for the over 12's and was divided into five teams who competed against each other. Team captains were Cynthia Sever (the oldest girl), Stephen Handfield-Jones, Douglas Myres, Peter Chalk and Sam Ellis. The latter was keen to do a bit of organising himself. Gradually the team system disintegrated as children began to invent their own games and expressed a wish not to be organised.

Informal sing-songs in the stern of the ship are fondly remembered. Although the crew organised one every evening it was at 10 p.m., after the children were supposed to be in bed and therefore the Rhodes scholars' sing-songs were much appreciated. The Rhodes men taught the children the words and tune of O *Canada* and one of them played a banjo. Although bed-time for all unaccompanied children was at 9 p.m., few had left the singing by then.

We little imagined the sadness and heartbreak experienced by some of the Rhodes scholars. We assumed they must be happy because they were going home. As one of them wrote: 'About this time [the summer of 1940] we began to receive a bit of mail from the American consulate. The general suggestion seemed to be that we should go home. The Warden [of Rhodes House] put no compulsion of any kind on us but he was frank to explain the situation was grave and in his opinion it would be wise to go. I think I can speak for all of us when I say no one wanted to leave. A million roots had to be pulled up. A romance or two had to be rounded off *tempo presto.* Oxford wins a person in such a quiet way that he hardly realises what has happened until he has to leave.'

When word got around that there was a famous film star on board some of the girls made an expedition to the first class deck where they were actually received by Elizabeth Bergner.

Talks with members of the crew were instructive. The Chief Engineer was happy to speak about birds to a receptive audience of Jean Chalk, Helen Somerset, Cynthia Sever and Ann Spokes. An exerpt from Ann's diary reads:- 'He was a very nice and friendly man with blue eyes. He told us a lot about sea birds and showed us a stormy petrol (sic) which they call 'Mother Carey's chicks'. Then he told us about the gannet colony that is getting smaller and smaller.'

Birds of some sort were always with us, delighting especially the poetical ones. Felicity Hugh-Jones wrote:- 'The Fulmans and Kittiwakes which I thought had left us have come again, dancing on their swallow-like wings, and showing their white breasts to the setting sun.'

The boys were more interested in inspecting the guns and on one occasion Peter Spokes and the two Ellis boys, Sam and Robert, were on the bridge turret being shown how one of the guns worked by some sailors but then, wrote Peter at the time:- 'We saw the captain coming up one stairs to make an inspection that he makes every day...so we had to scoot down the other stairs so that he would not see us as we are not allowed to go up there.'

Felicity Hugh-Jones wrote in her diary/letter:- 'The stewards, waiters and sailors are very nice, one of the sailors played a nice game with us but he had to stop soon - he said he wasn't allowed to, also the chief-master was at hand - he looks like those bread rolls you get at Keble. There is a nice sailor who read my label and told me what I knew already which was I was Welsh, and called me "little Miss Jones". I think he was Welsh himself.

Towards the end of the journey some of the girls started a craze which might have shocked North Oxford. They staged wrestling matches which soon brought enthusiastic audiences of adults who viewed them from the upper-class deck above. Joey Burn and Ann Spokes began and were soon joined by the Ellis brothers, Sam and Robert. The contests took place on an ideally-suited hatch cover, about three feet off the ground, the size of a boxing ring, beneath a good viewing area. Boys and girls wrestled against each other, the girls usually winning. When the girls had to leave to bath the babies, boys fought boys. It became a popular sport and Ann, though proud of the fact that it had all been her idea, was not quite sure whether her parents would have approved of mixed wrestling.

'It wasn't rough really,' she wrote to her parents, 'and I am sure if you had been there you wouldn't have minded us doing it and it was good exercise. I was very stiff in the arms this morning after yesterday and have a few bruises on my arms, elbows and legs.'

It is likely that this mixed sport was not approved of by all the adults. The next evening the girls were told that they could just sit and watch when a man brought some boxing gloves so that the boys could compete in 'proper' two-minute rounds of boxing.

The icebergs

The event which is still remembered even by people who were small children at the time was the sighting of icebergs. They had a beauty and magic which few had imagined. When a large one was seen, Ann Huckstep (née Macbeth), who was almost seven years old, remembers 'someone telling us that there was a fairy and a dragon behind it.' Felicity Hugh-Jones was having a bath when the first iceberg was sighted (at 3.30 p.m. on Tuesday, 16th July) but she wrote:- 'as it was only a speck I missed nothing. When I came on deck another one was there - this time it was very big, though it was, according to the Captain, ten miles away. It was a beautiful mountain of glistening white ice, with the blue sky above and the sun shining, thus increasing the brilliance of this beautiful object. There was a big hole in its side. They were going to fire at it to break up its cruel beauty, but much to the disappointment of the children it was decided not to as there were so many babies. We saw a few more and some big bits of a broken up one - just like a shark with a heavy head and forked tail.'

On 17th July, after having sighted land 'we saw a few more icebergs,' wrote Felicity, 'one shaped just like a gigantic submarine.'

Mrs. Ethelwyn Goodwin recorded:- 'We saw icebergs today - many small 'growlers' and one terrific one like a turreted castle. The excitement was incredible especially as it was supposed to be unusually large - the lights on it were very beautiful.'

Jenny Newman (née Hugh-Jones), aged 9, rushed for her camera when one of the icebergs came into sight but by the time she had collected it 'the iceberg was just a small blob on the horizon.' She still treasures this small old snapshot, now unfortunately a little worse for wear with the crease running through the spot.'

Time changes

The ship travelled about 350 miles a day and clocks and watches were of course adjusted as the ship moved westwards. The hour change did not suit everyone as Felicity Hugh-Jones wrote at the time:- 'The very young babies were quite frantic, waking up at the most queerest hours yelling to be fed.'

Mrs. Goodwin, one of the mothers, wrote:- 'For the last four nights the clocks have been put back an hour, so the children wake earlier each morning. Whisperings begin at 5 a.m. Rodney [five months] wakes at 3.30 a.m. for a feed - and from 5 onwards the noise increases - culminating in breakfast. Whew! The worst meal is tea when the children are getting tired and the final climax is before going to bed - each shouts louder to make himself heard. In this noise I try to feed the baby!'

There were at least a dozen babies under two in that resricted space, no bigger than the smallest college dining hall.

Although the food was good, with plenty of fresh fruit (kept in iced containers), in the early days there was never enough food for tea. Then the adults and older children were asked to have tea at 3.30 p.m. and the younger children and mothers at 4.45 p.m.

'Finally,' wrote Mrs. Goodwin, 'Mrs. Burn went to the Chief Steward and suggested that we went to help cut bread and butter in relays to ease matters - as so many stewards were off duty then. I went in the first day and we have all been tickled to think what Oxford society would think of some of its "wives" cutting amongst the stewards in the pantry.'

Land sighted
At 10.30 a.m. on Wednesday, 17th July we sighted land - first Belle Isle and then Newfoundland in the distance. In relief, Mrs. Goodwin wrote to her husband:- 'Well, darling it seems as if the sea journey is going to end successfully for today we passed through the straits of Belle Isle and went along the coasts of Labrador and Newfoundland. The St. Lawrence estuary is beautiful - very much like the Highland lochs - with little hamlets and white cottages - sometimes high mountains.' After the long time at sea any sight of land would have been welcome but the spectacular scenery was an unexpected joy for both adults and children. One of the latter on whom it made an impression was Peter Spokes (aged 12) who wrote home a few days later:- 'Here and there you would see a clearing in the wooded high hills that came right down to the river. In these clearings you would see small settlements of wooden huts, about 20 altogether. In every one of these settlements you could see the spire of some sweet little church towering above the roofs of the little huts.'

As we neared Quebec Dr. Fulton took the opportunity to cable home to announce our safe arrival in Canadian waters. The news, received in Oxford on Saturday, 20th July, was naturally greeted with great rejoicing and the holding of some informal celebrations.

QUEBEC

The longest day
Although the original plan was for the *Antonia* to sail up the St. Lawrence to Montreal, there was a sudden change of plan when orders were received instructing us to land in Quebec instead. This was said to be because the ship was needed elsewhere and a quicker turn round could be made. The party was, therefore, woken at 5.30 a.m. on Friday, 19th July and asked to be packed ready, after a breakfast at 7 a.m., for disembarcation. Immigration officers came on board at 10.30 a.m. and an early lunch was served at 11.40 a.m. It was not until 3.25 p.m., however, that the ship tied up in Quebec harbour.

Our arrival alongside the quay was unforgettable. As the ship moved into place we were greeted by the cheers and catcalls of about a hundred British 'tommies' who soon broke into a rousing song of welcome. Many of us will remember their rendering of 'roll out the barrel' for the rest of our lives. As we lay alongside the dock they not only told us that they were members of the King's Own Yorkshire Light Infantry but that, having brought internees over, were going home soon. Then they threw cents up to us and, judging that half-pennies were the rough equivalent, we threw ours down to the soldiers. After one had thrown up a newspaper to Dr. Fulton he showered down some toffees. It was not until 9 p.m. that we actually went ashore. By then many of the younger children, after a tea of beef, bread, butter and milk, had been in bed for several hours, though fortunately not undressed. They were then roused to be taken off the ship with the rest.

Ellie Vickers (née Bourdillon) remembers 'seeing the first red-coated Mountie on the dockside - we had arrived.'

Ann Huckstep (née Macbeth), whose seventh birthday it was, writes about the arrival:- 'Shock, horror, people on the quay were speaking French. I had expected an English-speaking country.'

Next came the inspection of our luggage by the customs men. We were amused when the only question many of us were asked was whether we had any firearms in our suitcases. After a chalk mark was scribbled on the bags we were given a ticket-receipt so that we could claim them on arrival at Montreal railway station. Our first experience of transatlantic vocabulary was when we learned that these were in fact called 'baggage checks'.

Some of the luggage was mislaid and was found in the wrong section. To identify theirs the Oxford party had been allocated the letter 'X' for Oxford but as most people also had their surname's initial letter on their luggage confusion was inevitable. Wendy Clarke recalls 'the compassion of a real live Mountie when [her] brother's luggage was lost.'

The next new word we learned was when we boarded the train and took our seats in cars, not carriages. A welcome supper was served and the train finally left Quebec for Montreal at 11.40 p.m. Because of the Spartan conditions and the excitement of the day most of us did not go to sleep until well after midnight. 'Very late' wrote Ann Spokes in her diary, 'for little children who had been up since 6.30 a.m.'

The train, which had twenty-two coaches and one engine, was the second of two specials. It was what was known as *colonist car* accommodation and had polished wooden seats. Fortunately, pillows were handed out and most of the younger children were able to lie full length along the seats. Ann Spokes remembers Charles Florey sleeping soundly with his head on her lap, whilst some of the older boys slept up top on the racks. Wendy Clarke recalls the journey:- 'Lying across wooden seats and heaving brother back on the slippery surface every time our 'special' pulled into a siding.'

'It was a rather dirty train' wrote Felicity Hugh-Jones, 'and let out fearful youlls and yells on approaching a station'. What was then strange and dreadful soon became the familiar 'mournful woo-woo sound' now remembered by Felicity.

On the train, people began to wake up about 6 a.m. and we arrived in Montreal at 7.15 a.m.

MONTREAL

We were news in Montreal. Having left Oxford with no publicity because of security restrictions the children delighted in the novelty of being greeted by photographers and reporters.

Peter Spokes (aged 12) wrote at the time: 'We were met by many reporters who took our photos and asked us questions. I did not have anything to say thank goodness as they wrote it down all wrong.'

The Montreal *Daily Star* reported that Dr. Franklin had told reporters that the party would probably stay at the Royal Victoria College for a few days until papers and photographs were all in order, and that a Committee of Americans in Montreal were co-operating with the Canadian University staff in looking after all the arrangements.

15-year-old Sam Ellis, whom Dr. Franklin had called his adjutant and who had helped him all the way over, was reported by the *Star* as 'marshalling families on the station platform, telling them not to worry about their baggage and acting the sang froid of a seasoned traveller'. 'We had the dickens of a mess with the customs in Quebec,' Sam was reported as saying. 'The baggage was not put under the proper initials and we were searching all over the place for lost bags.'

Inevitably children were quizzed about air raids although few of them had had any experience of them other than going down into shelters when sirens wailed. Sam was reported as saying:- 'We didn't go to any shelters, in fact some of the old ladies don't get up when the air raid warnings are given because if they got up and came downstairs they would probably get pneumonia.'

'I'm not sure I like your trains very much,' a six-year old girl apparently told a *Star* reporter. You know there's very little privacy on your trains. Now in England we have compartments and...'

'Betty, another girl broke in [continued the report]:- "You mustn't say things like that. People might be fond of their trains here, you know - besides they have ice-water."'

Felicity Hugh-Jones in her letter home:- The trouble when we first arrived was the Press. They kept on making us pose for pictures and [they said] the most funny things about us that we expected to see Indians jumping out of the corners.'

Wendy Clarke recalls the warm welcome as we boarded the buses. 'Somebody shouted: "Tell them to send all the kids they've got. There's room for them here."'

On arriving at the Royal Victoria College at McGill University we were met by the Principal of McGill, Cyril James, and some members of his staff. Also present were representatives of Yale University and Swarthmore College, Pennsylvania.

After the deprivations on board ship life at the Royal Victoria College seemed luxurious.

'It was a relief to have bedrooms after those tiny cabins,' wrote Felicity Hugh-Jones in her letter home. 'There were many Red Cross nurses and nice girls in yellow overalls who are a great help in looking after the very young children. There is an immense sand pile, a room full of toys for everyone from pull-along toys to the most complicated plane kit made of balsa wood; also a lovely gym full of the most complicated gadgets and last but not least an excellent kitchen. There is no such thing as white bread, let alone the horrible dry stuff we had to swallow on board ship. Tea is also unknown; children and grown-ups alike drink clean, fresh milk which seems to be almost as abundant as water in Wales.'

Ann Spokes, writing home, praised the equipment and medical care:- We have shower baths here and lovely wash basins, washing sinks and ironing boards and everything we need. The medical attention is good. Tonight [21st July] they have a night-nurse on duty all the time. It may sound silly but quite a lot of people have been sick and a few have high temperatures. I suppose it is the change in the weather which upsets people.'

The weather was warm - like a heatwave in England - and the indicator of a giant thermometer outside in the street opposite the college exceeded 80 F at midday.

Mothers with their children shared rooms and Ann Huckstep (née Macbeth) recalls a 'hot cramped room for our family.' Although siblings shared if they were girls, as did brothers, sisters and brothers were given single rooms next to each other and found the accommodation spacious.

The Warden of Royal Victoria College, Mrs. Grant, had supplemented her staff with members of the Junior League, Red Cross, Boy Scouts and nurses. On the night before our arrival they had waited some hours for us before being told to go home and return at an early hour for our train. The Boy Scouts carried in our luggage and later worked the lifts which we soon came to know as elevators. They were friendly boys and it was not long before we were exchanging information about our respective countries. We were as eager for information about Canada as they were about England. It was not easy to help them as they knew so much already. Ann Spokes wrote in her letter home:- 'One Scout even knew the population of Birmingham which was more than I did,' although she was born there.

Looking back on those action-packed hot summer days in Montreal it is hard to believe we only stayed four days there. We were taken up to the top of Mount

Royal by the kindness of the Rotary Club and visited large stores, including Morgans where a lady at a piano played *There'll always be an England* as the boys came in, recognisable by their school uniform blazers and caps. Wendy Clarke remembers 'the sound of bagpipes when the Black Watch marched past outside the college.'

On the Sunday afternoon the whole party had a picnic lunch in the University Park, sitting in circles of our own age groups where we were handed food in 'grab-bags'. When people crowded to the railings to watch us eat we felt like monkeys at the zoo, especially when we ate the bananas provided for us.

We felt like monkeys at the zoo.

We were more pleased when some girls came round to the College to ask us for our autographs. We were also approached in the streets by people who wanted to speak to us. Fourteen of the girls went to a bank where the cashiers patiently changed one sixpence or a shilling which each of them presented in turn to

Most of the children of the Oxford party on the steps of the Royal Victoria College, McGill University.

enable them subsequently to buy a stamp at the post-office for their letter home. We were impressed by the fact that, although we did not do it, one could go all round Montreal in an open tramcar for about ten cents.

Girl students at McGill, who resided during term-time at the college, came in every day to serve the meals and organise games for us. Besides popular outings to swim, sing-songs were especially enjoyed. We were each given a small community song-book which had on its first page in this order:

God Save the King
O Canada
The Maple Leaf for Ever,

but which also included *Old MacDonald had a Farm* and *Mademoiselle from Armentieres.* Among films shown to us was one of the recent tour of Canada by the King and Queen.

We all had our photograph taken on the steps of the college on the Sunday, 21st July. Some families, however, had already left for Toronto and other destinations in Canada where they were due to stay with friends and acquaintances. Despite our quarantining in Oxford one boy, who had filled a last-minute place, had already contracted measles. Others, because of minor infections, were also forced to remain behind in Montreal while the rest of us prepared to leave for the United States.

JOURNEY TO THE U.S.A.

July 24th, 1940 was, for many of us, a historic day. Few then knew of the hard work behind the scenes undertaken on our behalf by our hosts at Yale and Swarthmore. An account of their efforts has appeared earlier in this book. The coaches left McGill at 9 a.m. for our 10 a.m. departure from Montreal railway station. Most of the older children well remember that enjoyable train journey, entering the USA via St. Alban's, Vermont. Reporters boarded the train and the Dragon School boys, in particular, had no trouble in answering their inevitable question: "What do you think of America?", this despite the boys having only seen it from the train windows for about an hour or so. Experience of Hollywood films enabled them to give what the boys assumed were perfectly satisfactory accounts. Photographers also stalked the train and Ann Spokes noted in her diary that Stephen-Handfield Jones had five photographs taken of him and was interviewed twice.

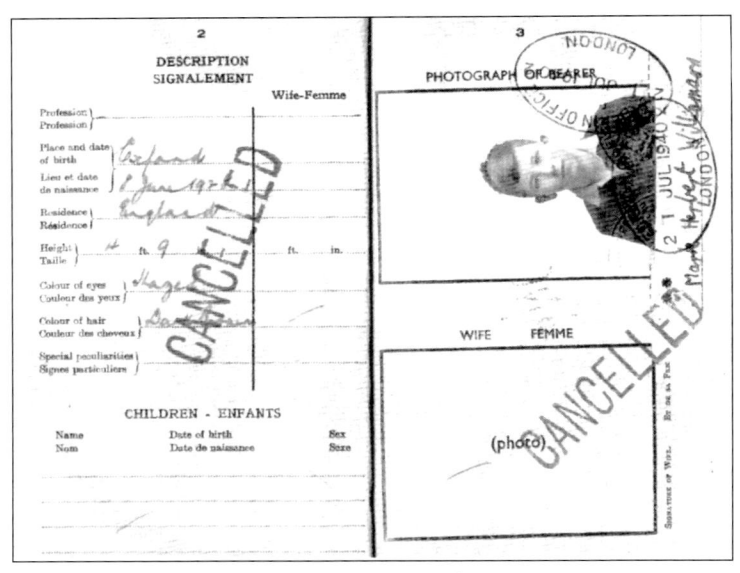

Example of a 1940 British passport.

It was evening by the time we arrived in New Haven where several hundred people waved and cheered us from behind some temporary barriers. The local newspaper, *The New Haven Evening Register,* recorded our arrival and captioned two photographs:-

*REFUGEES FIND NEW HAVEN IN LAND
HOLDING PROMISE OF PEACE*
and
*ENGLAND'S NEW GENERATION HERE
TO LIVE AS AMERICANS*

Once we had boarded our buses people came up and shook our hands through the windows. They also described us as refugees, a term we did not like. In another article in the same paper, headlined *'DRESS OF BRITISH REFUGEES HERE SETS THEM APART FROM U.S. YOUTH'* the writer had not only noticed the long outer coats, grey trousers and the longer 'short pants' of the younger boys but he was obviously fascinated by our summer footwear. 'Outstanding among the articles of clothing,' the writer continued' were the shoes worn by the youngsters - they had on sandal shoes of all possible shapes and styles.' Jackets with school insignia 'emblazoned on the pockets' were seen as unusual but so also were the 'natural colour straw hats to protect them from the rays of the sun and this was just as true of the boys as the girls.' Singled out for particular attention was the 'tremendous' one worn by a small girl on top of her pigtails.

Mothers and young children were taken to stay at the Children's Community Centre whilst the rest were boarded at the Yale Divinity School. The journey at an end, children were parted from other people's mothers who had cared for them on the journey. Felicity Hugh-Jones Arnott writes:- 'Looking back I realise now how little I noticed the care that was taken of us, or rather how much I took for granted. One of the mothers, Evelyn Phelps-Brown, who had her own children to care for was also responsible for us with, who knows, what cares on her mind already. I hope I thanked her at the end.' This goes for many of us.

Welcome To America!

Oxford evacuees arriving by train in New Haven, July, 1940.
Courtesy of the *New Haven Register*.

THE DIVINITY SCHOOL

Yale Divinity School in New Haven was home for the majority of the children in the Oxford Party until hosts were selected and homes found for us. We did not know at this stage whether we would be going to Swarthmore or remaining at Yale but, in any case, some of us enjoyed ourselves here so much that we were reluctant to leave. Hardly any of us children were aware of the fact that Mr. Byron Hacker, the Director of the Children's Center (sic), and his staff of assistants, were undertaking their investigations during this time, matching up children with the most suitable hosts and deciding on the allocations. During their stay at the Divinity School children were observed and sensitively interviewed to make sure that placements were as successful as possible.

Yale Divinity School Dormitories

Young Americans, New Haven residents or students at Yale who were still there in July, looked after us and were known as 'Counsellors'. Some were senior girls at Prospect Hill School where some of the older English girls later joined them when term began in September. We were well organised and all of us wore labels indicating our names, houses and room numbers which we tied onto our clothes with a coloured ribbon. It was a time of learning and exciting activities.

Many of us remember our first experience of fire flies, sparkling in the dark, but Wendy Clarke also recalls:- 'Fire sirens waking me to fear at night.'

Felicity Hugh-Jones Arnott still remembers 'the exotic sight of blue jays and the swarms of Japanese beetles.'

The application of mosquito oil was a nightly ritual, not only sprayed on ourselves but on the windows. Nevertheless, some children were badly bitten. Ann Spokes, writing in her diary at the time, was 'glad that I've got pyjamas on as there isn't so much space to bite.' It was perhaps indicative that one of the words in a charade we acted later was 'mosquito'.

An outing to the seaside at Madison beach was a particular pleasure, despite sunburn, especially for those who were driven there in a 13-year-old open-topped car called *The Yellow Peril.* Returning in it, with the wind in our hair, at the end of a perfect day, was an experience many of us still remember. We learned to play baseball and basketball or watched films - 'movies' of course. Keen tennis players were glad to be able to play on the Divinity school courts at any time of the day and badminton was another popular game. There was a further invasion of the media: this time news-reel men with 'talkie' equipment who interviewed half a dozen children. The older ones put on a play and, on another occasion, a group of older girls held a night-time feast in the grounds which consisted of biscuits, grapes, crisps and ghost stories.

Felicity Hugh-Jones, in a letter home, wrote:- 'We have plenty of things to do…We play with a hose in the orchard most of the time when we are not sunbathing, playing, swimming, reading, eating (meals mostly consist of fruit, milk and ice cream) and sleeping…If it weren't for the fact that you both aren't here it would be heaven.'

Playing with the hose was a favourite occupation, there being no swimming pool at the Divinity School and only a small one at the Children's Center. The under-twelves preferred to take all their clothes off before running through the water. Not everyone had swimming things because the Party's 246 heavy trunks were still in Montreal and did not receive clearance from U.S. customs until well into August.

The 26th July, Venice Baker's birthday, was memorable for a surprise birthday cake which not only had ornaments on but a musical box inside it which played *Happy Birthday to You.* Robert Ellis also had a cake for his birthday on 2nd August and it was at such parties that we tasted new varieties of ice cream and drank coca-cola for the first time. At the Children's Center there were also birthday cakes, and Ann Huckstep (née Macbeth) remembers them 'for my sister Helen and Kate Duthie who were both aged two on 10th August.'

All the children at the Children's Center were medically examined. His mother remembers Adam Raphael, aged 2, astounding the pediatrician by looking up at her face and remarking: 'You have violet eyes.'

'You have violet eyes'

Wendy Clarke recalls 'tea parties to be looked over by prospective hosts. At least it seemed that way. Going to tea in a beautiful home - three Steinway grands and Toll House cookies. "Would we like to live there?" "Yes please."

All the Counsellors were fans of the Republican Wendell Wilkie who was later to challenge Franklin D. Roosevelt for the Presidency. Coming from England we had never heard of Wilkie and were pro-Roosevelt, which we pronounced with a long 'oo' as in 'shoe'. Ann Spokes wrote in her diary that at last: 'We were able to find someone who was in favour of Roosevelt who could tell about him because we heard so much about Wilkie and everything bad about Roosevelt.'

As no one had heard from their families for three weeks an exciting event on 30th July was the arrival of our first letters from home. Some surface mail was received that had only been posted on 14th July and air mail sent on 19th July.

THE OPEN DOORS:
NEW HOMES AND FAMILIES

By the end of a fortnight children began to leave the Yale Divinity School to stay with their new families. Ten children and three mothers travelled to Swarthmore in Pennsylvania, eleven miles from Philadelphia, where Dr. Aydelotte, President of the Association of American Rhodes scholars, had been finding homes for Oxford and Cambridge children. He was a former President of Swarthmore College. This small group who travelled southwards stayed at Carson College, an institution for girls from broken homes, before being placed with local families.

The response to Dr. Aydelotte's letter, soliciting aid, is summed up by Rhodes Scholar Vaughan writing in the magazine *The American Oxonian* that summer:-'I suppose you must have shuddered, as I have many times, to think what may befall sleepy old Oxford if the Dorniers and Junkers find their way there, as well they might, in search of the Morris works at Cowley. The letter which came the other day from Dr. Aydelotte, soliciting aid from Rhodes men in helping to evacuate families of Oxford and Cambridge children, seemed to bring the war into very sharp focus...I believe a great many people in this country would welcome the opportunity of expressing sympathy in a direct, concrete way, after having sat helplessly by and listened to the radio reports of happenings abroad.'

In the same publication, Paul Swain Havens wrote:- 'In common I know with a number of you we replied immediately to Dr. Aydelotte's appeal for homes in this country for women and children from British Universities. A mother and daughter were at once assigned to us, the necessary affidavits cabled, and were momentarily expecting their arrival. But to our disappointment we had word that they were delayed by measles. One had almost forgotten measles among all the other dangers in contemporary England.'

Because it was high summer and numbers of hosts in the New Haven area were away on holiday or at their summer places, some children remained longer at the Divinity School. Others, like the Baker girls, resided temporarily in other homes until their official family returned.

It was a wrench for children to have to leave what was for many of them their first experience of a happy, mixed residential setting and where competitions, closely fought out between the whites and the blues, were reaching their final, crucial stages. A party had been arranged for the weekend and some hosts felt that they needed to prise their new charges away. There was, however, a tactful invitation to both children and their hosts to return for the party - a popular move typical of the kindness and consideration shown to us.

By 8th August there were only thirty children remaining at the Divinity School: about one Counsellor to every two people. A happy arrangement was then made for Counsellors to take friends of those already settled to pay short visits to them in their new homes.

Some of the larger family groups were allocated rented accommodation in New Haven. The Bostons and Macbeths, for instance, shared a house in Coldspring Street for a while, making a group of two mothers and six children in all.

Even some of the younger children can still recall the exact moment of meeting with their foster-parents. Daphne James Dunkin, who was ten years old, remembers 'the day our new "mother" came to collect the two of us.' Ann Spokes can picture still the blue, wooden-sided station-waggon in which she met Beecher Hogan, who had been waiting outside in it while his wife collected her from the Divinity School.

She was sad when, in the course of time, the car was replaced by another.

Helen Somerset (now Lock) whose older brother had remained behind in England, wrote:- 'Early in August Dan and Louise Darrow (both doctors) took me into their family - four daughters and a baby son - and the experience of life as an American began.'

For some of the children there was not only the necessary adjustment to foster-parents but often the acquisition of a brother or sister for the first time. In some cases this was a smooth and easy process; for others it took a little longer.

'I would like in these pages,' writes Heather Champion (now Dr. Heather Ashton) 'to pay tribute to my American sister, Mary. Suddenly presented with an alien sibling of the same age, who was treated as an equal in the family, who shared her room, her clothes, her friends and who (because of the difference in educational systems) was far more advanced in such important matters as Latin and hockey. Mary never ever, by word, deed or gesture evinced the slightest sign of jealousy. There must be few children in the world with the capacity to welcome so open-heartedly a cuckoo in the family nest. It may be sufficient to say that Mary, after a successful career as a biologist (and the mother of three children) is now a Deaconess in the Episcopal Church.'

Peter Spokes (aged 12), who was due to go with his sister Ann to the Beecher Hogans, was one of the unlucky ones who was in the second batch of measles victims. It was a surprise to him as he had suffered it once already in early childhood. The other children at the Divinity School, though sorry for him, were annoyed for fear that they too would now catch the disease. If they had known what it was like to be incarcerated in the grim isolation ward of the unimproved New Haven hospital they might have been more sympathetic. Because of strict hospital rules, Peter's meeting with his new foster-parents took place in bizarre circumstances. The Hogans were told that they could see him if they were completely enveloped in white sheets.

It was fortunate that Peter was not of a nervous disposition and showed no fear when these two strange ghost-like figures, looking like members of the Ku Klux Klan, approached his bedside. He could see nothing of their faces although slits had been cut in the sheets for eyes.

The Hogans had no children of their own and, in any case, what could even an experienced parent say at such a moment? C.C. Hogan's sudden inspiration to ask:- 'Would you like some ice cream?' broke the ice.

There were more offers of homes than there were children - probably why so few went to Swarthmore- and not all the hosts were given exactly what they expected. Barbara Falk, who had travelled with her two-year old daughter, Anne, and the unborn John, was collected by her hostess, Dr. Jackson. She remembers the arrival at her new home.

'July, 1940. Dr. Jackson's housekeeper opens the door to 'Doccy', holding Anne's hand, followed by the noticeably pregnant Barbara.

"Here are our guests," Doccy says cheerfully.

"But Doctor, you said an adolescent boy," was the guarded response.

Doccy smiled benevolently as always and put a protective arm round Anne:-

"This was the nearest they had, Margaret" and, turning to the horrified Barbara, "perhaps there will be an adolescent boy one day."

The English Children
by Margaret O'Neill Romagnoli
"Jim, do we have room for four more?" Mother's voice could be heard all over the considerable first floor of our old house.

Such a question in most families would be answered with a second question "More what?" but not in ours. Mother meant did we have room for four more children. I listened in amazement as my father, without even getting out of his favourite chair, replied: "I should think so but I don't know if I could really afford to buy more clothes."

My parents already had six of their own children, two in college, one in graduate school, and three in grammar and high school. There never was enough money to splurge on anything even though we always lived in elegant houses and had rather first-class friends and parties. We three older ones were poised for departure for the fall semester and yet not quite. It was a rainy day in late August 1940.

It isn't hard to remember; fifty years isn't so long when the year you are remembering was so changing, so much the end of everything we had once thought would be our tomorrow: finish school, get a job, get married, live happily ever after in a world without war. 1940 was our last full year together, ever, as a family. It was my last year of growing up. But, Mother's question and Father's answer gave us a new beginning, a step into today that some of us have been able to hold on to.

Our family, the O'Neill family of Lakeville, Connecticut, was instantly bigger, more complex, more different, and more full of life than ever before or since for that matter. The curiosity on our part knew no limits. Some could hardly wait for Mother to get off the phone.

"Four more!"

"Gosh, aren't six enough?"

"I am not giving up my room!"

"Do you suppose they're girls?"

Mock tragedy set in briefly until one of the older boys suggested they might be 'older' girls and then great relief spread across their faces. Mother went right on talking politely, standing at the wall phone which was situated for all to listen to, at the foot of the curved Victorian staircase, in the wide hall.

Finally she turned to us: "Well, we're going to have four English children staying with us." In the rush, interrupted by a myriad of questions, she told us about the new additions. With five brothers, I suddenly had three step-sisters and a stepbrother. My youngest brother Paul was elevated to being grown up, my eldest brother John became even more adult. It still doesn't seem quite real.

The four children were indeed brother and sisters: Felicity Hugh-Jones, 12, Jennifer, 9, Martin, 4 and Katherine (called Ziggy) 3.

One of the Yale Committee had called Mother just to see if she knew of any Catholic family that could take on four siblings to keep them together, at least for a start. Mother leapt at the chance herself.

Had she forgotten the days when the whole bunch of us had the flu simultaneously? Surely she hadn't forgotten the tug of war to get six off to school on time. How could she do this, some of us wondered.

And my father, who was grand at reciting poetry but pretty terrible at games, skating, being anything but a very large loving presence, how in heaven's name could he take on any more duties?

The older boys who hoped for older girls were momentarily disappointed but we all truly welcomed the 'English children'.

On arrival they stood clumped together in the big hall, the glass-paned door of which framed their outline with the lake beyond. They looked at all of us, very solemnly, the eldest holding onto the smallest who looked as if she'd never smile again. Not forlorn, just shocked into silence.

We viewed them with great curiosity at first and then with enormous care and love. They weren't ours, so they must be protected. They were like borrowed treasures to be handled gently. How many times when Mother heard a thump upstairs, she'd send one of us running by uttering one phrase: "Oh my, do run up and see if they are all right, what they are doing."

It had been some time since parental urgency surfaced so frequently. I could not grasp the depth of the children's anxiety or what they felt at the loss of their parents' presence, how overwhelming the fatigue must have been, the looking out for each other in their group plus 125 other children, children of the intelligentsia. At Felicity's age I had cried my eyes out on being delivered to an Aunt 40 miles away and here she was - grown up, pushed forward beyond her years. Last year she told me that she was so relieved to have the baby-sitting burden lifted she felt she was soaring, weightless. My Mother, Aunt Edith to the children, was Felicity's saviour. She could lean on Mother and to her, Mother was not a Nanny but a great surrogate. After a while Felicity's smile came back, her laughter, and she became a little girl again. Jennifer, perhaps by nature quieter, didn't say an awful lot in the early weeks but you knew she felt our curiosity all around her. And she was curious about us. Finally there came a day when curiosity turned to real affection and she blossomed.

With a 'baby' in the house, we all took turns to see

if the little ones were covered at night, wanted a night light in the hall, had said their prayers. We discovered there is more to prayer than the words or a wish. It was the continuity of it all that seemed to help.

How we all fitted in the house was the reason we were there in the first place. My father had a penchant for big houses and this 1880-ish house had a servants' wing where the two big boys, John and Jamie, could keep their mess to themselves. Hugh, the third boy, went to share the two younger boys' huge bedroom. There was a certain amount of grumbling over this and protesting but in the end, once school started and they all were driven off for 8 a.m. assemblies there wasn't much time for crabbing.

I had a compact little room with a closet big enough to hold my grandmother's huge Victrola which I played for the English children. Their sleeping quarters were divided up into two rooms across the wide hall. One of their rooms connected with my parents' room. When there was a sick child in the house, that was where he/she got to stay, to be watched over at night.

There were "bathrooms galore" as father explained to all and sundry: the lovely old house had been a boarding house for a short time before we bought it. On the main floor there were two living rooms, a library for my father, a magnificent dining room and a kitchen with a table for eight and a laundry wing. The latter was a huge joke, the most jammed-up space in the house, unworthy of its door to the garden. It was the dining room that Felicity reminded me of the last time we met. It was the focal point each day with its table that could and did seat 18.

We were fairly nice to each other at that table while the children from England were with us. They were a precious loan to my parents, generous, willing, sociable parents who began to treat their own children more like suitable young adults. We were growing up after all. But mostly it was the English who were nice. They made the American adolescent boy a fairly clumsy and noisy creature but viewed with love. All of the English children put up with questions from us. This included some pretty idiotic ones such as "What are you going to do on the Fourth of July? Bring down the flag?"

Nobody, however, touched their accents. Being children of a Speech Professor (argument, debate and drama were his forte), we might have but we didn't. I now think that their maintaining idiom and pronunciation was their only defence. Their personae were protected a bit by remaining, at least to us, very British. We in turn learned how to poise knife and fork the English way instead of all that crossing back and forth the Americans do. The English learned to recite poetry with the two youngest brothers and when it came to Chistmas with the snow deep around my parents saw to it that they had the accoutrement for Connecticut winters.

Mother also found time to take the children to friends who'd lived in England and had children so that the bridge to America seemed less long.

Margaret O'Neill Romagnoli

The new parents 'for the duration' wrote re-assuring letters back to their children's own families. The Hogans, who had taken in Ann and Peter Spokes, for instance, wrote:- '...They have been here a week and seem quite at home now. We have placed the health of the children in the hands of the best pediatrician in New Haven...

'I am trying to think of the questions you might ask, and trying to answer them!...We want you to know that we consider ourselves trustees of your son and daughter - and as we have no children of our own, they will be a son and daughter to us until you send for them...If there is anything that you particularly want us to do for the children - or any idiosyncrasies of the children that you feel we should know about - or special foods that you feel they should have - I wish you would tell us. And in the meantime I want to assure you that they will be well taken care of - and if it is in our power to make them happy then they will be happy.'

A Swarthmore foster-father, Hugh F. Denworth, who was caring for nine-year old Hazel Rankin, wrote to her father:- 'Hazel seems to have adjusted very easily to her new surroundings, and does not show any ill effects of the weeks of travel and temporary residence. She meets each new condition when it arrives and does not seem to worry. She has won her way into the hearts of our family, and we shall do our best to guard her and love her during her stay with us, and send her back to you in good health with happy memories. We shall take her along to our pedriatrician for a thorough examination before school starts. We are turning over to one of our leading orthodontists the information concerning the regulation of her teeth.'

In his next letter he asked Hazel's father:- 'We would greatly appreciate any suggestion or help you can give us so that we may make Hazel's temporary home as healthful and happy for her as possible. Please feel the greatest freedom in writing us of any concern you may have or of sending suggestions for us.'

IMPRESSIONS OF AMERICA
An *Anthology*

*****

My American family moved to a house near Brandywine Creek in Westchester County, Pennsylvania, while I was with them (for six years). This was the site of the famous battle in the American revolution, a battle which the American rebels won. A relic of the fight, an old cannon, was preserved in the garden of the house.

'What was this cannon for?' I asked in my youthful ignorance. 'To drive the British away.' was the answer. 'Well, it wasn't very successful, was it'? said I, as I straddled the cannon with my American siblings.

This remark became a family joke and is still retold to the grandchildren of my American family.

Heather Ashton (Dr.)
née Champion

*****

My own destination was Toronto where my host was an acquaintance of my parents. I remember a meal and delicious 'honeydew' drink in a restaurant of that name near the station while waiting to be collected by our hosts. I had unfortunately caught an unpleasant infection on my face, presumably from blankets in the Liverpool assembly hall. However, despite this, and all our very 'English' accents and habits, we were shown outstanding generosity in Canada. Free schooling, endless hospitality in homes with amazingly tolerant families who treated myself, anyway, as one of them.

The only financial support my parents could send was the international stamp coupons.

One summer holiday I joined the Ontario Farm Service Force and worked by the day or week for farmers who needed extra help for crop harvesting, strawberry hoeing, etc. On a day off two of us, greatly daring, hitchhiked to Niagara Falls. We were awestruck. 'My' family had a summer cottage at Muskoka where I joyfully learned to sail a 14ft dinghy, and found that 'Ivory' soap floated when taking one's bath in the Lake! There were also two happy visits to summer camp in Algonquin Park with canoe trips, balsam beds and blueberries - we <u>were</u> lucky.

At the end of three years school, I joined old friends in the U.S., trained as a secretary and worked and travelled for another three years with a voluntary organisation in the States. Again, I was very lucky and made lifelong friends, though six years was a long time from my family, for all concerned.

Ellie Vickers
née Bourdillon

*****

Our American hosts and hostesses were extremely kind, and opened their hearts and their homes to us. American schools were a bit of a surprise to those of us who'd been in segregated British ones with uniforms, lots of rules and strict discipline. American schools were co-ed, the hours were longer, and I was suddenly (in Grade 7) faced with memorizing the Constitution of the United States and the amendments. Unfortunately our class was studying the American revolution, so we Brits felt somewhat personae non gratae. I remember the teacher discovering that 'My country 'tis of thee' had the same tune as 'God Save the King', so she asked the other British girl and myself to sing the latter to the class. Up we stood, but Paq and I had forgotten the words and I can't hold a tune. The class must have been impressed.

Clothing was different too; we wore plaid skirts to school instead of gym tunics, and ski pants, snowshoes and ear muffs in the winter, and even little boys wore long trousers.

Foods were strange and so were the words for them. Our 'aunt' once asked us if we'd like crackers with our lunch and we looked for those very English treats - to discover that in America crackers were something rather dull to eat with soup. 'Icing' on the cake became 'frosting'. 'Biscuits' were 'scones' and 'sausage rolls' were 'pigs in the blanket'. We were introduced to corn on the cob, hot dogs and hamburgers (they had not reached Great Britain then) and to the ice cream delights of popsicles, fudgesicles and Eskimo pie.

To us becoming Americanized the war was far away. Our mothers went and sewed and knitted for British War Relief. We wrote letters to our family back home and received censored ones in return. Sometimes sentences were actually cut out. We tried to imagine what had been written in the spaces. We sent food parcels back to Britain, and I received my beloved Teddy bear forwarded on, and enclosed with it was a miniature gas mask, doll-size: a reminder of the days when we had carried gas masks every day to school.

After one year in New Haven, my mother returned to Britain and I went to a new family. Within that year my foster father was transferred to Chicago, and there I met no other British evacuees. My new school had a predominantly German population, and every week in current events we were shown news reels of the war. (Note: this was the pre-television era.) The bombing raids on London and the devastation scenes were frightening. Would the same thing happen to Oxford? Was that why we'd been sent away? Herr K. (our German science teacher - really Mr. K.) was keen on air raid drills (in Chicago yet!) and had mock smoke and fire and casualties and general alarm. I don't know which produced more nightmares - the news portrayal or the 'actual' thing in school.

Bobby Franklin
now Elizabeth Symon

*****

Hartford, Connecticut

I remember Alastair, Helen and myself reunited, staying with foster parents for the duration. A happy American childhood. School, 1776 and all that, saluting the flag, skiing, skating, summer camps, comic books. Good friends.

Ann Huckstep
née Macbeth

*****

Life in West Hartford, Connecticut

Skiing
The older ones skied in the back garden. One day I was allowed to have skis put on and I stood on the slope and was most upset that I did not slide. I did not try skiing again until an adult.

Proper School
I remember when at five [1943] I could, at last, go to the big school with the older ones. I was in the kindergarten class and, yes, we did learn to kiss the flag if we ever allowed it to touch the floor.

Reading
We only started to learn to read in first grade [1944]. We did not get scores or any numerical class order, but there were the 'Reds', 'Whites' and 'Blues'. This I now imagine was supposed to be more democratic, but I certainly knew the 'Reds' were the best at reading, as I was to tell my grandfather on return to England. No British sense of modesty or understatement were taught in first grade!

Helen Macbeth

*****

School was an enormous co-ed High School [in Hamden, Connecticut] where I was the only English pupil and an object of much interest! It was certainly different and a lot of time was spent discussing customs, food, weather and words - it made one think, and explain things that everyone had always known before.

Leisure activities were clearly defined - lots of snow, skiing and skating in the winter and sailing, swimming, picnics and camp in those reliable hot summers.

The War seemed far away and I longed for letters from home which often took weeks to arrive. Until Pearl Harbour the Americans either had an indifferent attitude or were definitely against being involved. The papers had news from London in one column and from Berlin in the other. The apprehension about being dragged into the conflict, however, completely disappeared after the Japanese attack, and even the isolationists were then 100 % in support.

Helen Lock
née Somerset

*****

February 1941 in the Yale Teaching Hospital. An excited voice is heard outside the door of Barbara's room. 'Nurse! Nurse! Come and see. There's an English mother in here. She doesn't have a formula. She breast feeds her baby. Did you ever see that?'

Barbara Falk
(Mother of Anne and John)

*****

I remember being asked to a party by the officers of HMS Furious, which was on a visit to Wilmington, Delaware. It was only for children - British children - and no grown-ups were allowed on board. We had to show our invitation as a pass; it was held on 20th December and I still have the invitation. We were shown the film Dumbo, but my sister Isabel was frightened and I had to take her out of the room.

Susan Berl
née Lawson

*****

A certain amount of sentiment softens the memory of that [first] year. So far I had always been 'the eldest', with all its burdens of being a good example and now I was safely in the middle of a large family with five older brothers and an older sister, godlike creatures all, who took us skating and taught us to ski and let us play in their tree house and live a noisy exciting life. Rather like something one had read out of Louisa May Alcott.

In the years since I've felt at worst guilt at our good fortune and at best gratitude for an example of how one should treat the stranger at the gate.

I know I was homesick at times, but more for the place we had left than the people. Perhaps it was a defence mechanism that turned the parents (who wrote regular loving lettters to try to keep in touch with us) into 'God-bless-Mummy-and-Daddy' icons whose portraits by Ramsay and Muspratt we took everywhere with us.

Felicity Hugh-Jones Arnott

*****

After an experience of the seventh heaven in Howard Johnson's (ice cream parlour) I remember being sick on my mother's lap on a car journey.

Bobby Burn

*****

I remember the five years absorption into the wonderful family of John and Perry Lee. There are so many and wonderful memories it would take a book to tell. Suffice to say that Anne and I became sisters of Jack, Puss, Nan and Tony and have remained so ever since.

Daphne Dunkin
née James

*****

Peter Spokes (right) with his new foster-cousin, Vic Tyler.

A letter home
August, 1941

My dearest husband,
I am a little sad as I have had no letter for ten days… I got one from Mother with a note from…Duncan[her brother] in. The latter's letter hurt rather:-
> *'Don't you think it is high time you started doing something for our war effort instead of gadding about the States on one glorious holiday? We hear a lot of what American women are doing in their spare time to help, but all you seem to do is park your children on some kind of long-suffering person and flit about the country having a good time. I take a very poor view of it and I am sorry to see we have a drone in the family.'*

Blast him. It is hard enough to make other people understand that these invitations away are made by friends who think they are helping the British cause by entertaining English mothers over here to help pass the time and to make them forget their aching hearts.

Also, I feel I want to see as much of American life as possible - one day I hope to write a bit of my experiences, and to do this, to progress mentally, one must live among the people, travel, listen and observe. A drone indeed! I am never idle. I have written an article for the British press which I do not suppose they have ever printed, a lecture on *'England in War Time',* made garments for the Red Cross to send to England and hope to do 12 and have nearly finished your first pair of socks. Olive has often said: 'Don't your eyes ever get tired with writing and sewing?'…

But I expect a lot of ignorant folk must think it dreadful our being over here. That is the reason I want to get home for I do feel sometimes that I am shirking my responsibilities even though a mother with children has to consider their welfare as her first job of work.

Confound him - I never meant to write like this but had to let off steam having half an hour ago received his letter. Comfort me a bit.

Ethelwyn Goodwin
(Mother of Richard and Rodney)

*****

I recall on one of our visits to New Haven, the daughter of Mr. and Mrs. Lovett (for all of us the ultimate host and hostess) had a tight schedule to get to the railway station. We could see the car stuck in a traffic jam and the policeman at the centre of the road just continued to let the traffic flow in the opposite direction. Finally, my mother could stand it no longer and went and had a word with him. He promptly obliged by reversing the movement, my sister and I were convinced that our mother had saved the day.

There were not many English people down in that part of the world [Nashville, Tennessee] and the early summer of 1941 found us christening the Vultee Vanguard aircraft for Britain. It was a big event for which Wendell Wilkie, then running for President, came. Washington Post was played as we took our place on the stand. Elizabeth, being the elder, actually broke the flask which, for the first time ever, contained liquid oxygen. Before the event there was outdoor luncheon at a plantation mansion and afterwards an evening at a Country Club where journalists got E. and me to make Chuchillian V-signs for our photograph.

Margaret Ewert

(Letter to a school friend in England, September, 1940)
Prospect Hill School, New Haven

Prep is called Assignments, Prep time is called Study and break is called recess. We have masses of time do do our prep in. We have a funny vicar for Scripture who winks at you...and stands with one leg over the back of his chair. He calls you Miss Chalk and Miss Spokes and so does the English teacher.

We play hockey, baseball, basketball and tennis and a soft kind of soccer. We don't have to play any games if we don't want to or come back in the afternoon at all except on Thursdays for English. We don't have gym.

Prospect Hill from the outside looks like a monkey house - worse than one in the London zoo - as it used to be one, but it isn't so bad inside with dark red floors and cream walls. It is awfully boring in some of the lessons.

There is no uniform in the school so you can wear whatever you like but we are not allowed to wear shorts. We play games in shorts but we are not allowed to go to the field in shorts but have to put skirts on over them until we get there. Perhaps they have a little excuse because the American shorts are so very short, almost as short as knickers.

Prospect Hill School, 1941.

No one stands up when a teacher comes into the room or opens the door and we always go out before the teacher and never stand up when we want to say anything. Everybody does their work and goes to classes; they want to get good marks at the end of term because they are going on to another nicer school afterwards.

Ann Spokes

*****

What impressions did the evacuation leave with me? I was an only child, and for me, it was a chance to live in a family setting. Supposedly any foster child, in wartime or otherwise, never feels completely at home with temporary parents, however kind and loving.

And here there was a different culture too, and for the first year and a half, the United States was a country that was neutral and not involved in our war. When the Pearl Harbour news came over the radio that fateful December 7th, 1941, I was the one who heard it, at a friend's house, and told my foster family when I returned. Their radio had not been on. In my relief that America was now 'on our side' how could I, a child of 12, be aware of their uneasy feelings, with a son of 17?

Bobby Franklin
now Elizabeth Symon

*****

Letters home

August, 1940

Our country summer house [in New Canaan, Connecticut] is in the middle of the country, you rearly (*sic*) wouldn't call it country you would call it Jungel. It is strange because wherever you walk somebody says 'look out for poison ivy'.

August 1940

I regret to say, Mummy, but Professor Moog [their host] plays the organ.' (aged 10)

August 1941

Please don't think I am forgetting you or do not like you, because I love you with all my heart, and more if there could be such. I can remember you all, your exprecens, your faces and your voices, without looking at photographs, and I am just hoping to get back to England.

Well, Tump and I are at the Willcocks having a super time.

Northampton, Mass   September, 1940

It is simply lovely going to school again. You don't do hardly any work at all. And, the work is easy. All the children are very nice. I have made a lot of friends already.

February, 1943

At 2 p.m. our class gave a Whashington Assembly. It didn't work too well because half our class was absent ... [Someone] was to memorize Lincoln's Gettysburg Address. She got it all muddled and got pink in the knees.

Diana Deane-Jones
now Armstrong

JOURNEYS HOME

"Opportunities"
The length of stay of the children varied from two years to six. People returned in groups or individually when they wished or at least when it was possible for them to obtain a berth. For security reasons a passage was usually described as a 'nice opportunity' or a 'special opportunity' to disguise its real meaning.

Parents at home signed forms releasing the United States Committee for the Care of European Children, Inc. and the foster-parents with whom the children had been living

from any liability of whatsoever nature with respect to the care and welfare of said child from, the time he/she leaves a port in the United States for the purpose of his/her return to us, including all responsibility for any dangers he/she may incur or injuries he/she may suffer on account of Atlantic transport from the United States to the United Kingdom.'

Many of those who returned before the end of the War had as dangerous a journey back as when they travelled across the Atlantic in 1940 and it was fortunate that all members of the Oxford party reached home safely. Many travelled home in convoys which suffered losses from enemy action or mines.

A group of boys were able to travel home courtesy of the Royal Navy. Alastair Macbeth writes: 'A new aircraft carrier, manufactured in the USA, was being delivered for the Royal Navy by a skeleton crew, and space on board was available for boys, but not girls. The ship (probably not yet named) docked in the Clyde and the boys were sent to Euston by train, arriving in the early morning of Sunday, 9th April, 1944, somewhat bedraggled after a night sitting up in the train.'

Boys returning home in a new aircraft carrier.

Hosts were reluctant to part with their charges while they still might face danger on the high seas or become victims of flying bombs in England. Mrs. Denis O'Connor, who had the care of Martin and Katherine Hugh-Jones, wrote a carefully composed letter to their father from New Haven in August, 1944. 'What is your reaction to Miss Case's interview with me in regard to the return of the children? Looking at it from here, it would not seem a favourable time. When the fear of invasion past, the children went back to England, more returned when the air raids subsided, but are they going back now that you are beset with the danger of the winged bombs or zombies as you termed them?

'Just how safe would it be for the youngsters at home now? You are there and would know better than me who are far away from the danger. While writing, Gabriel Heater is telling about the new secret weapon -the radio tank. However, you must decide. You must be torn between anxiety to see the lovely children of yours and the fear lest they encounter danger. It is difficult to use one's head when one's heart is pulling in another direction. Perhaps it will be over by the time a decision has been arrived at. Let us hope.'

Miss Marjorie Case, mentioned in the above letter, was Field Secretary to the Yale Faculty Committee for Receiving Oxford and Cambridge University Children Inc. of which Dr. John F. Fulton, M.D. and Professor Samuel B. Hemingway were Honorary Chairmen and the Reverend Sidney Lovett the Chairman. She took endless trouble arranging for the children to return home. Her attention to detail can be seen in an exerpt from a letter she wrote to the father of Martin Hugh-Jones which follows.

'It is good to hear that Martin is safely home and we can all rejoice. I hope he didn't have too much trouble with his luggage and was sorry that Mrs. Dayton didn't get that enormous doll in sooner so that it could have gone in his trunk. Mrs. Dayton will probably be writing you for your efforts in getting it to the Haslam-Jones but I want to thank you for delivering the little box to the Ewerts. It contained some little things which they left behind and which Mrs. Ewert wanted, and Mrs. O'Connor was kind enough to put them in.'

Miss Case's understanding of the needs of foster-parents in having to face the release of their charges and the joys of Oxford parents in being able to welcome their children home, is epitomised in another part of this letter:- 'In saying what I did in the cable about the O'Connors' reluctance I hope I didn't give much of an impression of urging you to let Martin stay. I rather wanted to have you understand something of the O'Connors' reaction ...Mrs. O'Connor took great pride and some joy though a sad satisfaction in getting Martin fixed up to go. She would not let us take care of any of the expenditures. We are so glad that you can have your child home.'

Marjorie Case 14th December, 1944

Both the American hosts and the Oxford parents owe a debt of gratitude to Miss Case for her work on behalf of the children. Her advice, based on experience, was a great consolation to those who had to part with the children and feared for their welfare once the journey home commenced. When she visited Oxford after the war, some of us were happy to be able to show her Oxford and take her to see Sulgrave Manor, the English home of the Washington family.

'I was too young to remember the voyage out, but had clear memories of the years in Swarthmore and the journey back. The *Mauritania* had been fitted out as a troop ship and it was the biggest thrill of my life to sleep in a canvas bunk. My mother tells me - I <u>wish</u>

I remember but in all honesty I don't - that I spent a good deal of the time playing *Authors,* an American card game on the lines of *Happy Families,* where each author - Tennyson, Shakespeare, Mark Twain etc. - had four books to be assembled, with young Conrad Russell and G.E. Moore, who was apparently greatly taken with this extremely small and precocious five-year-old. I'm not sure that I have ever equalled such heights since.'

Isabel Raphael
née Lawson

'As one of the older girls - I was 14 when we left England in 1940 - it was perhaps natural that I would suffer a sense of guilt because in war-time I had left my country for another. Because I was intensely happy with my foster-parents and hated the idea of leaving my school before graduation, I was tempted to stay on. However, I was equally anxious to return to England before the war was over. My guardians - as we called them (for they had been formally appointed as such by my parents) put no pressure on me to try to alter my decision.

I wrote home enquiring about vacancies in the services. I had always wished to join the WRENS (the women's arm of the Navy) and had naively assumed that I would be able to do so. My mother wrote back to inform me that at that stage of the war (November, 1943) there was nothing left but to become a cook in the ATS (the Women's Army) or a nurse. Having no desire whatever to be either I wrote back, in desperation, asking 'Isn't there <u>anything</u> else?'

The reply came informing me that if I were to obtain entrance to the University I could escape the horrors of cooking or nursing. This then was what I decided to do even though it meant staying on at school until June, 1944 and taking my college entrance exams. I had previously been spending much of my time painting and drawing but this was now discarded in order to study a year's Latin in one term and to be crammed for geometry and extra French. Those who had been evacuated to the States were exempted from the relevant entrance examinations to Oxford University if they had completed their school course with good grades and had been accepted by a reputable American college or University. On gaining entrance to Vassar I then only had to pass my college exams for St. Anne's on my return home. I was thus one of the few fortunate ones who was able to go direct from High School to University neither having to repeat a year's college or to attend an English school.'

Ann Spokes Symonds

'I came back in 1943 from New York on a Dutch cargo boat in a large convoy, with troopships and oil tankers on the inside for greater safety. The Battle of the Atlantic was almost won and we steamed along with constant vigilance from the escorting destroyers and planes above. Our ship's Captain stayed on the bridge day and night for over two weeks.'

Helen Lock
née Somerset

'The February of the Spring term (1944) I received a sudden summons: I was to go back to Britain via Trinidad and Lisbon on a neutral Spanish ship in company with Jean, another Oxford girl, and her young sister and some 30 other evacuees, plus a boys' school and their teachers. They had been evacuated to the States *en masse.* The crew spoke only Spanish, and when Jean came down with the measles, the only word we could understand was the nurse saying *baño.* I guess Jean had a lot of baths before she got better.

'After a day in Lisbon where we went sightseeing and found we could buy German souvenirs in the shops (I bought air mail envelopes that said *Luftpost* on them) we flew by Clipper to Shannon, Eire (in the honeymoon suite, five of us, all children) and thence by a smaller British plane to Croydon.'

Bobby Franklin (now Elizabeth Symon)

*****

Voyage Home
September, 1944
By Wendy Clarke
Total devastation of farewells in New York. Sailing next day in a tiny Mediterranean cruise vessel under the Cross of Lorraine, manned by Free French crew. Later discovered to be part of the largest convoy of the war, comprised of 2,000 ships. Travelled for 17 days at top speed of eight knots. Not a single book on board but every day something spectacular. A tornado, waterspouts and massive waves towering above the ship. Deck forbidden to the 20 passengers, but nobody really caring so two days' sheer bliss lashed to a stanchion, staring through walls of green and purple water. A tiny brown sparrow fellow-traveller.

A school of whales, so thick the sea was red with blood as the ship cut through them.

A calm and beautiful moonlit night when the ship was outlined with phosphorescence. Thoughts of U-boats inevitable but quiet conviction we'd be safe. Our nearest neighbour was sunk.

Nearing Ireland enemy planes bombing ships at the edge of the convoy. Our sole armament an AA gun, firing as I stood at the base of the turret.

Both Paris and Brussels were liberated during the voyage. Captain celebrated to insensibility and first mate followed suit. U.S. Navy radar experts locked them in their cabins and took over the ship for a few hours.

Arrived safely in Cardiff all the same.

*****

On leaving America in 1944
By Susan Berl, née Lawson
(who was 9 years old at the time.)
I remember it was very sudden. We only had 48 hours notice to pack up and get to New York so that we could sail for home on the Cunard liner *S.S. Mauretania.* This was a week before D Day. The ship had been used as a troop ship and for some reason was empty and they decided to send us home. I remember we arrived in New York City and it was very hot. Before we got on board our luggage was searched and an officious customs man turned the whole lot out onto the ground losing some marbles from a set of chinese checkers. He was American-Irish and anti-British!

We got on board and were shown into the First Class lounge which was full of hammocks put up for the troops. 250 Mothers and children were put in there. The bottom bunks had canvas put round them so that if it was rough the children would not fall out.

Before we set sail we were called up on deck and the Captain spoke. I will never forget this. He said: "We are sailing without a convoy. The first crossing without one. We are going to go fast. If any child falls over board we will not stop!"

It was very hot and we went the southern route. Every evening the boys got into the lower bunks and pretended to shoot each other over the edge of the canvas. The ocean was very calm and until we reached Ireland there was no rain. Coming up the Irish Sea the rain and mist came down. The crossing took six days and was the fastest so far.

We docked at Liverpool and it was cold and wet. We went into a shed with no roof owing to bombing and sat around the walls on benches, cold and miserable.

But I will never forget the kindness of the crew who gave every child a lunch box on a string containing an apple, an orange, sandwiches, a small bottle of coca-cola and a Hershey bar. Then we were put on a train with no glass in the windows and arrived later in London.

*****

December 1944
Father travelled to Hartford to fetch Helen and myself. My 6th grade teacher invited him to speak to the class, but I would not permit this, as I was so embarrassed by the English accent of this man who kept saying "jolly good".

Ann Huckstep
née Macbeth

*****

Father at Christmas
I remember when this amusing guy came to visit around Christmas, 1944. He was my father and he kept saying "jolly good", which seemed pretty appropriate for a visitor around Christmas. Isn't Santa Claus supposed to be jolly?

Helen Macbeth

*****

The Extra Bunk
By Ann Spokes

"The bulkhead was never intended to take another bunk; that's why it creaks."

This was the reply given to me by the Captain of the ship when I told him I was frightened about the safety of the bunk which creaked above my head. As a war-time emergency a third bunk had been fixed to the wall of the cabin. In this extra bunk was a six-foot man who had commandeered it because his wife, who slept in the bunk across the cabin from my bunk, wished to have her husband near at hand.

The *Erin,* a small merchant ship, left New York with a cargo of meat and twenty-one passengers during August, 1944 and took two weeks to reach her first port of call in Scotland. The journey was described by the shipping line as a 'nice opportunity' because it was war-time and safer for a passage to be so-called. The ship was so small that when I went aboard I thought she was a tender which would take us out to our boat. I wondered whether this 'ferry boat' was capable of crossing the Atlantic. Later on we were to discover that not only was she capable but that her size had certain advantages.

The cabins themselves were definitely 'nice opportunities' but because there were only a few of them families could not be given a cabin each and husbands and wives had to be separated. When the ship was in mid-Atlantic we heard that Paris had fallen to the allies and the U-boats, so the crew gleefully informed us, would be having their last fling. Night alerts became regular occurrences and we passengers spent many dreary hours in the dining-saloon waiting for the danger to pass. When sleep was possible it was in our clothes with life-belts at our elbows.

It was following several near bumps in the night that the man appeared in the bunk above me. When I was about to go to bed in the cabin which I shared with his wife, a face from the once-empty bunk above me suddenly appeared and he said:- "I hope you don't mind."

What could I say? A girl of 18 does not argue with such a man whom the other men had already christened 'The President'. I learnt the next day that he had obtained the Captain's permission, explaining that his wife needed to be comforted. The comments of the other wives - one with a tiny baby - are best not repeated. Every night for the rest of the voyage the bulk of 'The President' lay above me in a bunk fastened to a wall which was never intended to hold it.

At dinner on the first night 'The President' and his wife had already proved to the other passengers that they had influential powers. Before he opened his sealed orders the captain, just for fun, invited each one at his table to say where we wished to land. We each chose a port nearest to our home and when the orders were opened it was found that our destination was within forty miles of 'The President's' home, St. Andrew's in Scotland.

My own connections with the crew were not at such a high level. The Chief Engineer somehow discovered that I could type and directed me to his office where I copied lists of winches and other equipment in triplicate. He was a hard master; if a letter were omitted in error he would not allow two letters to be squeezed together; the whole list had to be re-typed. My payment was in kind: a cuba libra (rum and coca-cola) after each typing session and deck-tennis with a member of the crew, hand-picked by the Engineer. Despite the restricted space on board there was just enough room for a deck-tennis court. The fact that it was often awash in rough weather made the game more interesting.

I heard long afterwards that this little ship survived

the war. On this voyage her shallow keel saved her when we sailed over the mine which blew up the ship behind us. A morbid member of the crew commented: "There goes the first of us."

It was afternoon and we could see her burn. The alarm bells had rung continuously which meant fire but there was no fire aboard our ship, merely the thump of the explosion vibrating beneath our feet, which for one brief moment made us imagine we had been hit.

On the last night aboard, the oldest passenger, an eighty-year old Scotsman, celebrated in advance the return to his native land. He had made the mistake of celebrating prematurely some weeks previously when a 'wee drop' or two in port had been the cause of his missing his first 'nice opportunity' altogether. His midnight celebration took the form of a peculiar reel which he performed in and out of the cabins. Sounds of protest from the ladies' cabins drowned the thuds of the depth charges.

'The President' and his wife were not amused. But so long as the bulkhead was strong enough to keep 'The President' in his high position above me I had no fears. We landed in Methil, on the east coast of Scotland, and it took me three days to get home to Oxford.

(written in November, 1961)

*****

The Journey Home
The boat journey home seemed O.K. to me, even if we were sick one day and had apples with sugar on. I do remember standing on the stern deck with Daddy watching two great columns of black smoke, which were apparently from two tankers sunk by German U-boats.

Helen Macbeth

*****

January 1945
Returned to England after three weeks at sea, with the convoy being attacked in the Irish sea.

Ann Huckstep
née Macbeth

*****

The Return to England, August 1945: Recollections
By Neil Maidment
My young sister Jacqueline, my father in his British Army uniform and I boarded the *Queen Elizabeth* at the Hudson River Pier, New York on Tuesday 14th August 1945 for the magic voyage home to England. Magic because, although Jackie and I had been born in Oxford, we had been too young in 1940 to have had any memories of it at all. During our five years in the United States we had heard countless stories of England, of Oxford and of the strange impersonal war which had apparently been going on somewhere else apart from America.

I was desperately eager to get home and to see those Meadows of Oxford and the Colleges which my parents had told me about.

As the *Queen Elizabeth* sailed slowly out of New York Harbour, I stood near the bow in the wind and watched Staten Island go past on the port side. The words WELCOME HOME BOYS were painted on a huge sign along the nearby slope of the island. Strange, I thought, I'm going home too.

The ship was absolutely vast, particularly for a young boy. She had decks piled on decks, elevators with brass fittings, endless miles of promenades and passage-ways. She was still painted grey. It was her first publicly-revealed crossing of the Atlantic since she went into service at the outbreak of war, converted into a troop-ship from a luxurious Cunard liner.

Nearly all of the thousands of passengers were people in uniform, men and women. Many were British troops returning from the eastern theatre after years of combat or imprisonment, others were members of the United States military en route to occupied Germany. I remember there were several pretty American nurses who told me they were going to Berlin to care for the wounded Allied soldiers.

Because we were practically the only two children on board and British to boot, Jackie and I were in constant demand by the British troops who had not seen their own children for five years or more. Every morning, a group of soldiers would knock on our cabin door (I remember it was C Deck which I imagine was pretty posh in later days) and ask my father if they could look after us for the rest of the day. What a boon it must have been for him, getting rid of us kids ! The soldiers would talk and play games with us; they used to plait Jackie's pigtails. What fun we had.

On 15th August, the Emperor of Japan announced the surrender of his forces in the East - VJ Day. The whole war was over. The ship went mad with happiness, everyone was so excited and delighted. There were parties going on everywhere. I shall never forget the atmosphere of sheer exhilaration and good nature of that day and night; it will remain with me forever.

On 18th August, I had my birthday and that was another excuse for partying, presents and general good-will. I was loaded down with Hershey chocolate bars, packs of gum and enough life-savers to preserve the whole ship's complement.

We sailed up the Channel from dawn on Sunday 19th August 1945. It was a grey, cool day with drizzle and mist. I was up on the Boat Deck running from side to side in absolute amazement. There were ships of every shape and size escorting us and they increased in number as we approached the shores of England. There must have been hundreds of them, filled with cheering people. There was one large ferry, I remember, leaning over almost to the rails in the water because of the weight of passengers crowding her port side. There were boats with brass bands playing and people singing. It was all because that frightful war was over at last. Britain's finest passenger ship, the *Queen Elizabeth,* the largest and fastest ship in the world, was coming home in public for the first time. Everyone was bursting with pride, happiness and tears. Looking back now, I realise it was the greatest moment of national glory in my life. But then, I thought how appropriate it was that half the population of England should be turning out to welcome me and Jackie back home.

We berthed at Southampton. The Mayor and Corporation were at the docks, more bands played. The gangways were lowered. Soldiers ran down and many prostrated themselves and kissed that wet, oily wharf. Everywhere there was great happiness.

In 1971, I had been working in Hong Kong for three years when the *Queen Elizabeth* sailed up the east Lamma channel into the harbour. She had been purchased by a Chinese shipping tycoon with the intention of restoring her to her former glories as a cruise ship and a floating university. Months of refitting and repairs took place. Three days before she was due to sail in her new colours, a series of disastrous fires broke out on different decks. She sank before my eyes. The cloud of white smoke covered the whole of Kowloon peninsula.

Neil Maidment, Hong Kong, 18th March 1990

HOMECOMINGS

Separations from home and family, which had lasted from between two to six years, did not all end happily. Some parents were shocked and saddened to find that children did not easily slip back into the feelings, attitudes and loyalties they had had before they left. Most of the older ones who had been in their teens when they said goodbye found adjustment easier. They had been able to keep in touch by correspondence; going home was returning to at least some still-familiar places - even if former friendships had died - and picking up the threads was possible in time.

Settling in was not always the happy time parents had looked forward to for so long. Some younger children did not recognise or even remember their real parents and yearned for the 'mother' they had left behind and no one thought of preparing the parents for this. Nowadays one supposes that counselling would have been offered. It was not easy for the 'strange' child to settle back into a family as if they had never been away. And yet some parents could not accept that a child of theirs should show no immediate affection.

In some cases new siblings had been born who now had an equally important position in the household. Best friends had been left behind in America and the change to a highly-disciplined school was difficult.

The time children took to adjust was often, of course, dependent on their own background and personality. Those children who needed but a week to feel at home in America were often the ones who only took a week to feel happy again in Oxford. Those who had understanding parents who accepted that settling in would take time were the luckier ones. Those who admitted to being miserable abroad and who never really enjoyed their stay, were probably the ones who had most trouble relating to their own parents. One girl who had been unhappy in Canada, isolated from her English friends, said she never came close to her parents again after her return home.

There were also one or two children who, except for occasional visits, never returned. It was not that they did not love their parents but just that, in the course of time, they felt and believed that they were Americans.

There follows a selection of impressions, some contemporary, of home-comings.

For the younger ones the only home they could remember was in America. As Helen Macbeth points out: 'To the older ones, America was the funny place but for the younger children (who had left home under the age of two or three) England was the funny place.'

*****

Coming home
'I was in a daze, very tired even before the journey for we lost an hour of sleep anyway every day, we thought we were at Islip, we were at Oxford, and somebody was opening the door. It was about midnight, pitch black outside. I had just woken from a sleep or doze, I don't know which. Somebody had a flashlight. I saw Daddy and recognised him immediately. We all stumbled out of the carriage. I hugged and kissed Daddy. I was a great shock to them - so tall. Then I saw Mummy, but I did not recognise her. She has white hair and looks

very tired. I was dazed and could not believe it. Finally we got a taxi and arrived at Postmasters' Hall.

School
It is more like a reform school than anything else, terribly formal, ugh! A lot of people who were in my grade (form) when I left are still there. At first they treated me like a museum piece, now they have actually condescended to speak to me.

Diana Deane-Jones (now Armstrong)
From letters written in June, 1944, aged 14.

*****

'My brother's first words on my return to Oxford in September, 1943: 'He's a little Yankee.'

The taunt of 'Yank, Yank, Yank' at the Dragon School made me adopt an Oxford accent pretty quickly.'

Bobby Burn

*****

'It is hard to know if I remember this, because the story is often retold. Being six and a half on return I was missing front teeth. I had also gained a black eye on the boat home. I was full of true American self-confidence on Oxford station when, clutching my panda, I marched ahead of my father and Ann and went up to this woman and introduced myself as her daughter. Mother had been looking out for us, above my head. I did get the right mother; yet, I don't think that in America I could remember her. The sight of this 6-year-old tough must have been quite a shock for her.'

Helen Macbeth

*****

January, 1945
'English winter, rationing, school uniforms, 1066 and all that, Latin, French, American accents, a new baby sister. Home.'

Ann Huckstep
(née Macbeth)

*****

'Sometimes we felt this wondrous life [in the USA] would never end and then rather miraculously, we suddenly found ourselves back in England with our own father and staying in Trinity college in time for D-day. So we were home again and there to witness the stream of American Army trucks making their speedy way through Oxford City centre with supplies *en route* for the continent, helping us to final victory.'

Margaret Ewert

*****

'It was good to be home, but England looked shabby and the people, especially the women, tired and anxious. My American accent faded, and I learnt about rationing and English pounds, shillings and pence as I settled down as an undergraduate.' (1943)

Helen Lock
(née Somerset)

*****

'I don't think we talked much between ouselves about our experiences. Children tend to keep miseries to themselves. After the war the four of us were separated by boarding school and college. I don't remember talking to the parents much about it either; perhaps it was a reluctance on both sides. With relatives or new friends, guilt at my comfy war kept me quiet and how did one describe it all anyway? I felt outlandish enough with the smart American clothes and noisy American accent. The latter got discarded pretty quickly but the former were precious. I remember Jenny and I shared a new-look creation which shuttled between St. Anne's and Somerville depending on whose turn it was to wear it.'

Felicity Hugh-Jones Arnott

*****

'We were met by our parents in London. They had last seen us as young British children; we returned to them as American-style teenagers. It must have been quite a shock.

'London was blacked-out, and so was the train that took us back to Oxford. It was back to black-outs, yes, to rations of food and clothing and petrol, to Make do and Mend, to an all-girls school and uniform (I had to dye my American plaid coat navy blue and startled the gym teacher - I was 15 - by having painted toe nails), back to Latin and air raids. I had a tin helmet which I used as a door stop in my room. When the siren rang one night shortly after I'd returned home, I got up, put on the tin hat, and went back to bed. I thought the raid only another of Herr K.'s practices, and did not realise the need to seek shelter.

'Children from London had been evacuated to the safety of Oxford. My contemporaries wondered why I had gone to the States. But the choice had not been mine to make.'

Bobby Franklin
(now Elizabeth Symon)

*****

Some American hosts received, in due course, an illuminated address from Queen Elizabeth (now the Queen Mother) with a colourful royal arms at the top of the page. It read:-

"I wish to mark, by this personal message, my gratitude for the help and kindness you have shown to the children who crossed the sea from the United Kingdom many months ago. Since the early days of the War, you have opened your doors to strangers and offered to share your home with them.

In the kindness of your heart, you have accepted them as members of your own family, and I know that to this unselfish task you and all your household have made many great sacrifices.

By your generous sympathy you have earned the true and lasting gratitude of those to whom you have given this hospitality, and by your understanding you have shown how strong is the blood tie uniting all those who cherish the same ideals.

For all this goodwill towards the children of Great Britain, I send you my warmest and most grateful thanks.

ELIZABETH R"

'Fifty years on, although the memories are' as Felicity Hugh-Jones Arnott says, 'partly and almost too far away to recall, I don't think I would have missed it all for anything.'

'I realised how lucky I had been,' writes Helen Lock (née Somerset), 'to have spent those years in the United States, broadening my outlook and receiving so much kindness and generosity from everyone, especially the Darrows. We have exchanged many visits over the years, kept in touch regularly with letters and now our children have made contact too. It has been a lifelong experience.'

*****

'It would be interesting to see how many of us have come back across the Atlantic* to settle and raise our families; how many married an American or Canadian; how many have become citizens of their new country who might not have done so otherwise.

'I married an ex-RAF navigator who had trained in Canada in the war years, so for both of us, when we emigrated with our family in 1962, it was a return to North America, our wartime home.'

Bobby Franklin
now Elizabeth Symon

Ten of those who left Oxford in 1940 in 1990 lived in Canada or the United States. Ten live in Australia, New Zealand and other places outside Europe. [Ed.]

*****

'I suppose our family was exceptionally lucky with the emotional generosity of our foster-parents. Despite loving us as their own children, they nevertheless built up, even in me who did not remember Oxford, an excitement to go home and see a new sister, etc. I don't recollect that it ever occurred to me it might be a sad thing to say goodbye. Only as an adult was I to learn what it meant to my American foster-parents.'

Helen Macbeth

*****

This collection of memories of our war-time journey and the years which followed is dedicated to those trans-Atlantic foster-parents and their families who opened their doors and their hearts to us. Although invasion never came, it was a near thing and there are few of us who did not gain from our visit and live richer lives as a consequence.

We end, therefore, with some words from the daughter of one of the foster-families, Margaret O'Neill Romagnoli, (whose story, *The English Children,* appears earlier in this book). It was written after both she and the eldest of their visitors had married and had their first babies.

'Mother was still in touch with her English children. She never mentioned the hundreds of meals and piles of laundry. She only remembered those dark-eyed children. Her war effort made her a godmother, not a grandmother.

'Nowadays when things look a little empty around my house, I just think of that extended family and remember the soft voices, the clean accents and the pleasant ties that bind.'

*****

1947

When Ann Spokes graduated from Oxford University in 1947, her American foster parents from New Haven attended. In the photograph, outside the Sheldonian Theatre, are (left to right): Peter Spokes, Ann, CC Hogan and Beecher Hogan.